*+ l om you.
friend,
Kathleen*

Loving
Choices,
Peaceful
Passing

*Why
My Family
Chose* **Hospice**

Kathleen Vallee Stein

For information about this title or to order other books
and/or electronic media, contact the publisher:
Valleeview Publishing LLC
Monrovia, California
valleeview.com

Library of Congress Control Number: 2019907542

ISBNs: 978-1-7326202-0-9 (print)
978-1-7326202-1-6 (eBook)

Printed in the United States of America
Cover and Interior design: 1106 Design

For my husband, Paul Stein,
and my parents, Bob and Maryanne Vallee

"You'll drift apart, it's true,
but you'll be out in the open,
part of everything alive again."

- Philip Pullman, *The Amber Spyglass*

Contents

Author's Note

This is a memoir and a work of creative nonfiction. It reflects my recollections of experiences and my interpretation of conversations that took place. The conversations in the book are not written to represent word-for-word transcripts. I have retold them to evoke the feeling and meaning of what was said. Although my experience was profound and meaningful, I cannot guarantee that it will be the same for other families.

Acknowledgments

Many thanks go to Sarah Hunter, who inspired me to write from the heart, and welcomed me into her writers group, where I experienced a perfect blend of honesty, wisdom and unfailing tact. They are: Sandra Browne, Diane Corwin, Linda Crockett, Peggy Gregerson and Jane Hallinger.

My first readers were generous with their time and provided valuable feedback. They are: Carol Gilman, Hope Koncal, Karen Solzak Rice, Edie Taylor, and my brother, John Vallee. John's willingness to share the deeply personal letter he wrote to Dad gave greater insight into our family's taboo against expressing feelings.

I am abundantly grateful to Rabbi Arthur Rosenberg, who added immeasurably to the book by sharing his experience as Leonard Nimoy Palliative Care Chaplain at the Motion Picture & Television Fund where he works on a daily basis with families like mine. He beautifully describes in the Foreword that hospice is not a death sentence. The choice of hospice is an act of love.

I couldn't have gone through the hospice experience without my sister Anne Vallee Johnson, and her unwavering support for me, and for our parents.

Finally, I want to thank my husband, Paul Stein, for always encouraging me through my book's fifteen-year journey. He was my first editor and is the best husband in the world.

Foreword

Wに do we all want? That is a large question. I would venture to say that none of us wakes up each morning and hopes for a day of pain, loneliness, alienation and misery. Let's underline "pain." None of us wants pain.

In my work as the Leonard Nimoy Palliative Care chaplain at the Motion Picture & Television Fund in Woodland Hills, California, I daily meet people like Bob Vallee's family. They are filled with angst and empathy for a family member. They have just found out that medical science has a lot of "modalities" but are not equally concerned about the human feelings and existential concerns of people like you and me.

Bob was ill, very ill, and his treatments were destroying whatever quality of life was left. He could not swallow, could not eat solids and had terrible coughing fits when he tried. As his daughter Kathleen, author of this book, puts it, "If Dad had gone through another week of radiation he would have died a horrible death, and we would have missed that sweet memory, along with many other moments together. My sister, mom and I had the opportunity to say goodbye, each in our own way. As Dad's body began to fade away, I felt a spiritual connection to him that continues to this day."

Let me take a moment to state the obvious: We are all going to die someday. If our lives are solely about the how and when, where is the humanity? Are we just machines that fail? Of course not! Our days should be filled with the experience of being alive, no matter our condition. I suggest that life is not about avoiding death. It's all about how you live. How would you like your life to be filled? I hope with love, meaning, satisfaction, connection and building bridges that lead to forgiveness and acceptance.

In my trade we call that QOL: quality of life. How is the quality of *your* life measured?

For many people there is a point in the road of life where there is a fork. There are two signs posted at that juncture: **quality** and **quantity.** Just to be clear, I am speaking of those who have a life-ending or life-limiting diagnosis. God willing, you will have both quality and quantity for many years. But for others, the days become short, and the choice becomes one of "just one more course of chemo or radiation," as Bob Vallee faced, or "one more clinical trial," as a dear friend of mine faced, or "one more surgery," or another "one more." "Yes," the doctor says, "the side effects will be terrible. You will have nausea, probably lose your hair. You might sleep all the time and may not keep food down. But we may be able to buy just a little more time."

A little more time for what? More time to be sick? More time to sleep? More time to be in agony? More time for my loved ones to see me suffer? Less time to say *The Four Things That Matter Most* (from Dr. Ira Byock's 2004 book): "I forgive you. Do you forgive me? Thank you. I love you."

Palliative Care and Hospice are not about giving up. They are not about sending our loved ones off on an iceberg to drift in an endless sea in their last days. Palliative Care is a team approach to medicine where the doctor is one member of the care team. It includes nursing, chaplaincy, social work, dietary and on and on. We treat the whole person. And when a diagnosis of six months or less is given, then Hospice takes over with its holistic team to continue the support for a pain-free quality of life. In my experience I have seen people live longer and with better quality while on either, or both, Hospice or Palliative Care services. There are studies, such as in the *Journal of the American Medical Association*, which have published results showing how early Palliative Care enhances mood and quality of life.

As the Vallee family discovered, and Kathleen discusses in this book, Hospice is not a death sentence. The choice of Hospice is an act of love. Their choice to place a loved family member on Hospice services led to stunning moments of life. They had the time to finish their unfinished business, to cope with some family rifts, and love up to the very end of Bob's life.

To love is a verb. Verbs are action words. Some of the actions that are most important to convey your love to those you hold dear are: having an Advance Care Directive, choosing someone who knows your preferences to be your designated Power of Attorney, completing an Ethical Will, and always keeping the door open to those who care most about you. And let's not forget an early referral to either Palliative Care or

Hospice. In so doing, life becomes less about being controlled by the medical machinery of the twenty-first century and more about reclaiming your own humanity and that of your loved one. And isn't that the purpose after all? I love the thought often ascribed to Vivian Green: "Life isn't about waiting for the storm to pass … It's about learning to dance in the rain."

May we all learn to dance.

With joy.

Rabbi Arthur Rosenberg
Leonard Nimoy Palliative Care Chaplain
MPTF, Woodland Hills, California
July 21, 2018

Introduction

I WROTE THIS BOOK FOR FAMILIES who are facing a terrible choice. I'm not a doctor, nurse or social worker. What is contained in these pages is how my family faced my dad's impending death with acceptance, rather than denial. His passing was peaceful, on his own terms. But first, and most difficult, was accepting that he was dying and releasing him from the hospital's culture of cure at all cost. My dad lived his last days in the comfort of his own home, cared for by my sister and me. It wasn't easy, but we did it.

Doctors are slowly coming around to the idea of letting terminally ill patients go home to die, but most aren't there yet. Stopping treatment goes against the grain of the medical profession. My dad's physician did not suggest hospice, but when I brought it up, he helped us discuss it with my father and guided us as gently as anyone could. His precise words were, "It's best when the family decides."

Many people aren't aware of the Medicare hospice benefit. I know about it because I was Manager of the Health Insurance Counseling and Advocacy Program (HICAP) for Los Angeles County. HICAP helps beneficiaries understand Medicare and the benefits it provides. When I would describe the Medicare hospice benefit to seniors who were facing a terminal diagnosis, for themselves or their loved ones, they recoiled. "Oh, no! We can't do that. We can't give up!"

We never "gave up" on Dad. He was facing another week of radiation for non-Hodgkin's lymphoma. The previous three weeks had left him too weak to get out of bed and unable to eat. When the doctor suggested a feeding tube so Dad could continue the radiation, we found another way.

My father's last twenty-nine days of life were some of the richest of his eighty years on earth. I cherish the memories of caring for Dad, who faced his final days with courage, and remained a gentleman to the end.

Choosing hospice care requires tenacity and a strong will. If you don't think you have that kind of fortitude, don't worry, you'll find it along the way. You may have to reverse roles if it's your parent who is ill. I made decisions for my parents, in spite of their objections, and the next day they thanked me. When I looked at my elderly, frail parent, I had to stop seeing the authority figure who told me to finish my homework and go to bed at 8:00 p.m. He wasn't that person anymore, and I wasn't a little kid. I stepped up and did what had to be done.

This process isn't for the faint of heart, but it's worth a try. You can sit in the intensive care waiting room as your dad passes from this world, or you can take him home and sit with him by his bedside. You can watch your mom suffer more and more indignity in a hospital, or take her to the safety of her home. You can develop a relationship that you never dreamed of, or you can be a bystander to a terrible death.

It's far from an easy choice, but if your experience is like mine, it will be well worth it.

CHAPTER I

Circling the Wagons

AFTER THE THIRD WEEK of radiation, we knew the treatment was killing Dad faster than the non-Hodgkin's lymphoma, so we took him home to die. It was just the four of us: Mom, Dad, my sister Anne, and me. We circled our little wagon train, determined to help Dad die with dignity. It was a Herculean task, overwhelming at times, and we struggled to stay the course. But the alternative hovered over us during those harrowing days: Dad lying in a hospital bed, fed by a tube, radiation bearing down on his already battered body, killing him before the cancer could.

Beneath the turbulence of those days, on the bottom of the ocean, lay a deeper understanding of my dad. Taboo-breaking feelings were dredged up, and a fierce protectiveness toward my parents surfaced. My father's transition to eternity was peaceful, on his own terms, and in his own home. My memories of him today do not bring regret, but gratitude for the tender intimacy that only impending death can bestow.

I would never have imagined back in 1959, when I was nine-years-old and in the third grade at Whittier Elementary School, that my ferocious father would ever be a lamb. One day, in a darkened classroom, I watched him struggle to thread the 16-mm film onto the big wheel of the projector. His volunteer job was to show the "movies" for the school's annual social. The building was packed with parents and children who played carnival games, ate cookies the moms made, and watched cartoons. Dad's frustration grew when he failed to get the film to fit in the tiny slot. I could see the signs that he was about to blow, and I was terrified that he would swear in front of all these people. But at last the film snapped into place, the Mr. Magoo cartoon began, and I was saved from humiliation.

My parents, Bob and Maryanne Vallee, were married, over the objections of both families, on June 3, 1944. Mom's family didn't approve because Dad wasn't Catholic. Dad's family didn't approve because Mom *was* Catholic. The young couple married at City Hall in Milwaukee, Wisconsin, and raised their children unaffiliated with any organized religion. Black and white photos, taken after the ceremony on the steps of the courthouse, show a slender woman with hazel eyes and softly curled brown hair directing a million-dollar smile at her handsome new husband, a tall, bespectacled man, his hair combed back from his high forehead.

Their first child, Dick, was born nine months after the honeymoon, followed two years later by Anne. Although I never asked my parents directly why they moved with their two small children from Wisconsin (where their families lived) to Ohio (where they knew no one), I thought the disapproving relatives might have had something to do with it. After they settled in Findlay, Ohio, Mom gave birth to three more children: me, Jean, and John. John was born on Mom and Dad's twelfth wedding anniversary, June 3, 1956.

Mom said Dad was a manufacturer's representative, but he called himself a peddler. He sold power tools and other hardware items to retail stores in our home state of Ohio and in Illinois, Indiana, and Michigan. He left on Monday morning and returned on Friday afternoon. "Kids, Dad's home!" Mom would call out to us as Dad pulled into the driveway. That was our cue to make a quick mental inventory of what we had done during the week that would make him mad.

My parents built a ranch-style house in a new housing tract in Findlay, nine months before John was born. Since they weren't expecting Jean, who had been born three years earlier, John was a *really* big surprise. Unbeknownst to my parents, their new home was on a flood plain with a creek nearby that overflowed its banks on a regular basis and flooded the entire neighborhood. Our house was the only one with a basement, and when the floodwaters came, it filled to ground level—right to the top step of the stairs. After the water receded, Dad would pull all his tools from his basement workshop, dry them out in the sun, and then haul them back downstairs.

Dad's workshop was his refuge. He spent most of his time on the weekends making furniture for our bedrooms: a small desk, a dresser, or a bookshelf. The basement always smelled damp and musky. Lit by fluorescent lights in the ceiling, it had scary dark corners. When Dad started down the basement stairs on Saturday morning, I would get worried. Every week, one or more of his tools were missing, or moved from its designated place in the workshop.

"Goddamn it! Where is my hammer?" he thundered one such morning. "I told those damn kids to stay away from my tools . . ." I sat quietly at the kitchen table, trembling with fear. Then I heard my name: "Kathy!"

I had a one-in-five chance of getting nabbed, and this time I was "it," dead man walking, down the steps, one by one, scared out of my wits.

Dad's brown eyes bore into me, his anger like a bonfire, and I was about to get burned. "Where's my hammer?" I was standing close to him, but he yelled loud enough to be heard upstairs. "How many times have I told you not to take my hammer?" I was too terrified to answer, but I knew it was many, many times.

"Go find it!" Dad's temper was at full throttle and raw, naked fear jogged my ten-year-old memory. It was in the garage. I had been trying to nail two boards together and then figured out the nails weren't long enough to do the job and abandoned the project, and Dad's hammer. I tore upstairs, got the hammer, and ran back down the stairs, trying not to wet my pants.

I offered the hammer to him as if it were my first-born son. He grabbed it from me and said, for the one-hundredth time, "Don't take my hammer again!" Every time I had this encounter with my ferociously angry dad, I thought I'd learned my lesson, till the next when time he was gone, and I started a new project.

One of the neighbor kids had a dad who clapped his hands and said, "Good job!" if they did something right. We knew we wouldn't get such praise from our dad, much less applause, so we concluded there was something wrong with that kid's family.

When my brothers and sisters and I watched Ward Cleaver talk to the Beaver and Wally on *Leave it to Beaver,* we laughed. We thought the only kid that seemed real was Eddie Haskell, because he reflected our cynical view of the world, a view we had honed by living with our dad.

We had a good mother. Some of our friends had really mean moms, and their dads weren't much better, so we were grateful for what we had. Mom cooked all our meals and packed our lunches, cleaned the house, and did the laundry. She was a pretty good sport, and she kept her sense of humor.

On a sunny summer morning, a couple of wild ducks from Eagle Creek waddled into the backyard to see my sister Jean's pet duck.

"Mom! Moooom! There are ducks in the yard!" Jean, John and I were screaming at once. "They want to take Jean's duck!"

"Help me get them in the car so we can take them back to the creek." She didn't miss a beat.

"Mom! Moooom!" we yelled again another time. "There are pigs in the yard! They got out of the farmer's field!"

"Get in the house, they're dangerous!" Mom called out to us. There would be no pigs in Mom's car. The pigs slowly walked away, but Mom kept us in the house for a few hours until she was sure they were gone.

Then there was the time the newly minted driver, Anne, tried to back the car out of the garage, hit the storm windows

Dad had carefully mounted on the wall, and smashed them all. That time Mom was too stunned to speak.

We visited our relatives in Wisconsin infrequently when we were young and then less and less as we got older. Dick developed an attachment to our grandfather, Earl Vallee. He bypassed Dad and chose Earl as the man to emulate. He was enamored of Earl and Anita, our grandmother. After he retired, Grandpa renovated an old farmhouse in Cedarburg, Wisconsin, and transformed it into an elegant home. The white clapboard house rose from a fieldstone foundation. The pitched roof had dormers in front and back. The house stood at the top of a long, perfectly green lawn, with mature oak and maple trees in front and a small apple orchard in the back. It was filled with antique furniture and carefully decorated by Anita in Colonial style. My grandparents called the house "the farm."

Dick and I went to Wisconsin to visit our grandparents, by ourselves, when he was twelve-years-old and I was seven. Just flying on an airplane was heady stuff, but the elegance of my grandparents' house and their affluent lifestyle overwhelmed me. Grandpa picked us up at the airport in his wine-red Chrysler Imperial with a white interior. Dick sat in front with Grandpa while I sunk into the soft leather upholstery in the back seat. Grandpa pulled into the long driveway and drove around to the back of the house.

When he got out of the car, we followed him into the kitchen where the aroma of Grandma's delicately seasoned roast beef was a revelation. I had never smelled anything so tantalizing. The dining room table was set with delicate china in a floral pattern, with pink roses in the middle and sprays of ferns and white lily of the valley blossoms around the edge. I was awestruck.

"You're here!" Grandma exclaimed as Dick and I entered the kitchen. Her hair was perfectly styled, and her pearl necklace and earrings complimented her elegant dress. Even her apron was fancy, a calico print with rows of ruffles at the top and bottom.

"Kathy was afraid on the airplane but I calmed her down," Dick boasted.

"You are a good big brother," Grandma said.

"You shouldn't be afraid, Kathy," Grandpa said, a bit sternly. He had the same brown eyes as Dad, with the same intensity.

"I'm okay," I managed to squeak out.

The next morning I sat in the sunny nook of Grandma's spotless kitchen, while she spread strawberry jam on my toast. I was so overwhelmed by the house, my grandparents, and the food, that I was unable to speak.

"Do you like strawberry jam?" she asked.

"Yes," I said, barely above a whisper.

"Do you like school?" she tried again.

"Yes, I'm in second grade," I said, barely audible.

"Do you want to help me take out the trash?" Grandma asked. She was trying to engage me, but I wasn't making it easy. I was paralyzed with shyness.

Even something as mundane as an incinerator was elegant at my grandparent's house. It was made of red brick, with a heavy cast-iron door and a chimney. Grandma stuffed the trash into the incinerator and threw in a match. The paper burned quickly. Suddenly, Grandma spit at the heavy door, which had grown quite hot. Her saliva sizzled, much to her delight.

"Wow," I said. "Can I try?"

"Of course," Grandma said as she spit again.

"It's fun!" I said with a big smile. Finally, Grandma and I had bonded.

Dick was with Grandpa, describing all the chores he wanted to do. "I know how to run the riding mower," Dick said, eager to impress his grandfather. "I can clean the barn too. Or Kathy and I can help you take the trash to the dump." He was willing to work hard to please the old man.

"Start by mowing the lawn. Take Kathy with you," Grandpa said.

I ran over and jumped onto Grandpa's riding mower while Dick drove. First, we took a tour of the property, which had a large barn with an apartment upstairs, Grandpa's woodworking shop, and a corn crib, an old wooden structure that had been used to store corn decades earlier but now stood empty.

"I love it here!" I shouted over the roar of the mower's engine. "Can I drive?"

"Hell, no!" Dick shouted back. "You're way too young."

It was during that visit that I knew I wanted what Grandpa and Grandma had—a quiet home without the constant chatter of children and the messes they made. Everything in the house was fancy, right down to the soap in the bathroom. It was pink, with an elegant filigree design around the edges. Stamped in the center was *Sweetheart Soap*. When I lathered my hands, a delightful scent of roses filled the room.

When Dick and I went back home, we were both homesick for the beautiful, quiet, magical home where our grandparents lived.

Earl and Anita were not interested in having many grand-children. I found out after I grew up that they called Mom and Dad's home in Ohio "the baby farm." The disapproval of their son's growing family came to a head with Mom's pregnancy with Jean. Because they were afraid, my parents waited until she was born to tell Dad's parents that baby number four had arrived. And sure enough, Grandpa's response to the happy news was swift and brutal.

"Don't expect me to support all those kids!"

Earl left no doubt. Kids cost money, and he didn't think Dad was up to supporting them. Dad was humiliated and Mom was crushed. Jean was often ill in the first few years of her life. One very cold winter night when we were getting ready to go to bed, Dad carried three-year-old Jean, wrapped in a blanket, to the car. Mom and Dad took her to the hospital because she was having difficulty breathing after battling bronchitis for over a week.

"Go to bed. We'll be back," Dad said to the four of us. Dick, age twelve, was put in charge. John was asleep in his crib, so Anne and I went to bed and hoped Mom and Dad would be back in the morning. Mom said Jean was put in an oxygen tent at the hospital. Anne and I thought that sounded like fun, being too young to understand that it wasn't like camping.

I remember watching Jean when she was five years old as she ran back and forth from her bedroom to the bathroom during a bout of diarrhea when she had the flu. "Jean has diarrhea again," Mom told Dad on the phone when he called from Michigan. Jean overheard some of the conversation but only heard Mom say "die" and thought she was dying. She told me later she was terrified but didn't talk to Mom about it.

Jean missed three months of school in second grade because she had nephritis, a kidney disease.

She may have inherited her intense personality from our father and grandfather, or she may have been so scrappy because she didn't feel good for the first eight years of her life. But Jean took no crap—not from anyone, even Dad. When he yelled at me, I tried not to pee in my pants. When he yelled at Jean, she gave it right back, fearlessly. The two of them were like pieces of flint: The more they knocked against each other, the brighter the sparks.

Jean sat across from Dad at the dinner table on a Sunday night in midwinter after we had been cooped up in the house all weekend. The two grumpiest people in the family started to get on each other's nerves.

"Stop looking at me," Dad said to Jean, glaring at her. He had just complained to Mom that the pork chops were dry. We were all on edge.

"I'm not looking at you," Jean replied with a frown, her chin jutted out.

"Yes you are, stop it!" Dad yelled.

"I'm not looking at you!" Jean screamed.

"Look someplace else!" Dad said, yelling louder.

"Mom, may I be excused?" Jean got up from her chair before Mom could answer, shot Dad the stink eye, and marched out of the dining room. Then Dad took a beer into the living room, sat in his easy chair, and turned on the TV. The rest of us relaxed and furtively slipped pieces of our dry pork chop under the table to Speckles the dog.

When Mom was pregnant with John, Dad had a vasectomy. Earl and Anita were not as upset with baby number five because he was a boy. They were diehard sexists, and boys were just flat-out more valuable than girls to them. John played the baby of the family to perfection. He had a happy nature and a quick wit that could make a menacing older sibling who was about to hit him start laughing instead.

The only one below John was the family dog, a mutt named Speckles. Mom's constant refrain after Speckles came into the family was, "John, stop teasing the dog . . . stop teasing the dog, John . . . leave the dog alone, John . . . stop it!"

As each of us married and left home, Dad got more relaxed. The bathroom was no longer Grand Central Station in the morning. He converted one of the empty bedrooms into a neat and tidy office, and his tools stayed put. Mom and Dad went out to dinner a couple of times a week to give Mom a break from the kitchen. When the grandchildren came along, he was playful with them. They called him "Grandpa Bob" and weren't afraid. As he got more relaxed, Mom got more relaxed too. My parents and I enjoyed each other's company and entered a new phase in our relationship.

I understood Dad better and started to realize how much I was like him, especially in our need for tidiness and order. I had a bedroom to myself for only a few years while growing up, and it became my haven, like Dad's workshop. If someone went in my room and took something, I was as incensed as Dad was about his hammer. Talk about "birds of a feather."

After Dad retired, he and Mom left the home they had lived in for thirty years and moved to Prescott, Arizona. By then I had settled in Los Angeles, and my older sister, Anne, lived in Scottsdale, Arizona. Our parents, in their early sixties, were relatively healthy. Dad kept busy for a couple of years overseeing construction of his dream home, with a workshop adjacent to the garage that would never fill with water. After raising five children, Mom said all she wanted to do was sit down and enjoy needlepoint, reading, and watching TV—and that's what she did.

During those years, Anne and I got closer to our parents, not just because of proximity, but because we spent more time with them. They spent Thanksgiving at my house in Monrovia, California, and Christmas at Anne's home in Scottsdale. Dick, Jean, and John saw Mom and Dad infrequently, with two or three years in between visits, especially after they moved to Arizona. After the first family feud in 1987, it all fell apart.

It had started innocently enough when Dad sent all five of us a letter asking us to sign a legal document that consolidated his family's three trusts. Our signatures were required because we were beneficiaries. Anne and I signed and mailed the documents back right away.

Dick, Jean, and John refused to sign. They wanted to see to see the original trust, claiming that Grandpa was a very smart man and they needed to reassure themselves that Dad was fulfilling his intentions. The thinly veiled accusation was that Grandpa was smart and Dad was stupid. John changed his mind and signed, but Dick and Jean's intransigence was a bomb lobbed into what we had previously considered to be our distant, but basically congenial, family.

The battle lines were drawn. Anne and I were steadfast in our alliance with our parents, and Dick was the four-star general of the campaign against Dad. Dick and Jean's deification of Earl Vallee justified, in their minds, disrespecting their father. Mom knew there would be no winners in this conflict, not with her father-in-law's ghost so deeply embedded in the battle. She took a neutral position but it didn't help. John played both sides. Eventually Dick and Jean signed, but the damage was done.

We retreated to our respective corners and life went on until the summer of 1993, when Mom went for a checkup, and the doctor could not detect a pulse in her ankles. Her circulation was poor. Mom, a slender woman for most of her life, had developed a big tummy and wasn't motivated to lose weight. I will never know if the doctor suggested going on a diet and exercising, but I do know he recommended major surgery to increase the blood flow to Mom's lower extremities.

"She had a heart attack during the surgery, and they took her somewhere. I don't know where," Dad told me, his voice full of fear. I learned later that it wasn't a heart attack, but Mom had started to bleed unexpectedly during the procedure. The surgeon stopped the surgery and closed her up.

"I'll be there tomorrow, Dad. Where is Anne?" I said, chastising myself for not being there during the surgery. I had booked a flight for the next day. "She is still at her class," Dad said, and I shuddered when I realized he was alone. Anne was taking a class in medical transcription that morning and was probably on the way to the hospital. Mom and Dad had downplayed the seriousness of the surgery, so Anne and I weren't too worried. None of us thought there would be such serious complications, but I regretted that we weren't more careful to ensure Dad wouldn't wait during the surgery alone.

Mom spent the next three days on life support in the intensive care unit. Anne, Dad, and I waited outside the ICU, leaving only to eat and sleep. Anne left messages for Dick, Jean, and John, keeping them updated. John called back and offered to come if it was the end, but nobody knew if it was the end, not even the doctors. Dick and Jean did not call Anne or Dad back. Mom had probably told them not to worry, and they were unable to take in any information to the contrary. It was easier for them to conclude that Anne was overreacting and Mom was fine.

On the morning of the third day, the doctor said Mom needed a procedure called a sigmoidoscopy (a flexible tube, with a light on it, is inserted into the sigmoid colon). He thought some of her tissue might have died due to lack of oxygen during the surgery. In that cute way doctors talk when they describe unpleasant procedures, he said he wanted to go in and "take some pictures."

"Can I be there?" I'm pretty squeamish but had been through a colonoscopy and knew what Mom was in for. I wanted to be present, even if she were unconscious. "That's fine," he said as he walked away.

I got to the ICU shortly before the gastroenterologist arrived. Mom had IVs in both arms, with multiple plastic bags full of fluid hanging overhead on what looked like a hat rack on wheels. A nurse called the cluster of tubing that flowed from the bags into Mom's body "spaghetti." Occasionally Mom's eyes would flutter open, but I knew she was unconscious.

The gastroenterologist started the procedure, and I cringed. The smell in the room was ghastly. The doctor kept turning a little valve that released the gas and commented on how much there was. I leaned down close to Mom's face and asked her if she wanted me to swear for her. Mom never said anything worse than damn, or hell, so my offer to swear for her must have been liberating. Mom's lids lifted and our eyes locked. She nodded, signaling "yes."

I began to swear like a sailor: "Goddamn, son-of-a-bitch, holy crap!" Mom never used these words. They simply weren't part of her vocabulary, until now.

Given Mom's feelings about religion, I didn't offer to pray. She fought for survival in the best way she knew how, not by cowing and crying, but by crowing and describing in colorful language the indignation she felt but was unable to express.

"Bullshit, holy hell!" I was getting into the swing of it. The doctor and nurses didn't seem to notice. Or, if they did, they didn't care.

At last the procedure was completed. The doctor left, and I told Mom I'd go tell Anne and Dad that she did a great job. She told me a couple of weeks later that my swearing had got her through the ordeal. My mother and I had fought hard, and we had won.

The next morning Mom regained consciousness. The nurses let all three of us be in the ICU, suspending their one-person-at-a-time rule. Anne and I stood on either side of the bed, with Dad at the end, and said corny things like, "Hi, sleepyhead." Mom stayed in the ICU for a few more days and then moved to a regular room for another week. Anne left Dick, Jean, and John the good news on their voicemail.

During those long days in the ICU waiting room, Anne and I developed a relationship with Dad that went beyond drinking together during happy hour and eating meals in fancy restaurants. He leaned on us, something he had never done before. We sustained one another while Mom was so critically ill. Dad loosened his parental authority and saw Anne and me more as equals.

"I want to take you two out to dinner tonight," Dad said. "We need to celebrate, and I want to thank you for helping your mother and me."

"Can we go to Bourbon and Bones and get a big, juicy steak?" I asked.

"That sounds good," Dad answered.

After Mom got home, she had six weeks of cardiac rehab and looked better than she had in years. Dad was livid that Jean and Dick didn't reach out when Mom was in the ICU. The anger and resentment from the first feud were never resolved and remained in the background, like a virus in an operating system.

While Anne and I got closer to Dad, his angry shadow side festered. Dad felt Dick and Jean had disrespected Mom, and his anguish was expressed in anger. The three of them exchanged nasty letters. There was carnage, and no healing.

Five years later, in 1998, when Dad was diagnosed with colon cancer and underwent surgery, Anne left messages for Dick, Jean, and John from the ICU waiting room. John called her back immediately and also called Dad a few times over the next few weeks to check in. Dick and Jean did not respond.

Two years later, in August of 2000, Dad's diagnosis of terminal cancer was confirmed. By now we knew the drill. Anne and I were at the hospital, John responded to Anne's messages, and called Mom and Dad occasionally. Dick and Jean might as well have been on Mars.

Dad had five children: two estranged, one who wasn't estranged but wasn't close either, and two who were about to walk with him through his last days. My sister and I became a team and trusted one another. I'm not sure I could have done it without her.

Anne and I weren't close when we were growing up. I was a tomboy, and she was more of a girly-girl. I was a hard-boiled cynic, and she was more trusting. I would jump into things, and she would pause for a moment. Our temperaments didn't mesh.

One bitterly cold night in 1959, when I was nine years old, I went outside after dinner to play on the snow ramp my brother Dick and I had built a few days earlier. Our neighborhood, on former farmland, was flat. If we wanted to slide on our sleds, we had to build our own snow ramp. We rolled up several snowballs, pushed them together, and sprayed it with the garden hose to make it icy.

It was a moonless night; the only light was from the back windows of the house. I pulled on my snow pants, winter coat, boots, and mittens, and then begged Anne to come outside to push me off the ramp. Eleven-year-old Anne didn't want to go out into the dark and the cold. I begged and cajoled until she agreed, to "shut me up."

I got myself positioned in the center of the saucer sled at the top of the ramp. Anne gave me a big shove, and I flew off into the dark, holding on to the sled handles as tightly as I could. On the way down I hit a patch of ice, almost flipped over, then bumped up against a snowdrift at the end of our one-half-acre lot, out of breath and exhilarated.

"I made it!" I screamed with delight, lifting the sled up for my sister to see in the dim light.

"Let's go inside," Anne complained. "I don't want a turn. I'm cold."

I wondered why she wanted to go inside. The cold night air frosted our breath, and the icy ramp and adventure beckoned to me.

After we were long grown and had families of our own, Anne and I worked to help our parents through many illnesses and surgeries. In August 2000, when we faced Dad's terminal illness together, our different temperaments complemented one another. I don't think Anne would have hired professional help without Mom and Dad knowing about it, but she agreed with me when I did. I know I wouldn't have called our siblings to tell them about Dad and hospice, but I was glad she did.

There were no peacemakers among the seven of us—five adult children and two aging parents. No one told us to knock it off and get along, if only for Mom and Dad's sake. There were no pastors, no lifelong friends of the family, no favorite uncle or sensible great-aunt who intervened. My parents raised us far from our relatives, outside of organized religion, and with no close social network of any kind.

I didn't know how Dick and Jean would respond to Anne's attempts to communicate with them. Would they soften, or would Dad's terminal illness fail to thaw the thirteen-year-old ice? My sister and I cared for our father during his last days, with estrangement poised over our heads, like a sword.

We were faced with a decision when the doctor suggested a feeding tube so that Dad could be subjected to more treatment. I stood by his bed and looked at a suffering man. Continued radiation would make him suffer more, for no good reason. It was common sense time, and Dad was a very common sense guy.

His lips were dry and chapped. He was hungry and thirsty, but when he tried to eat or drink he choked, gagged, and then coughed for as long as twenty-five minutes.

"Dad," I asked gently, "would you like some ice chips?"

"That would be nice, Katrinka," he said. I had forgotten that he called me that pet name, and the memory came thundering back. I was about four years old, eating breakfast in the kitchen in Ohio. Dad was headed to the back door, on his way to work. He stopped, and his voice was playful when he said, "Katrinka, what does Tony the Tiger say about corn flakes?"

That was my cue. "They're GRRRR-EAT!" I proclaimed at the top of my lungs.

He had a big smile on his face. "Say it again, Katrinka." I told him, no less enthusiastically, "Tony the Tiger says they're GRRRR-EAT!"

He chuckled and went out the door. I will always cherish that moment when Dad and I remembered a time when he was a young man, and I was a small girl who made him smile with my Tony the Tiger impersonation.

If Dad had gone through another week of radiation he would have died a horrible death, and we would have missed that sweet memory, along with many others. My sister, Mom, and I had the opportunity to say goodbye, each in our own way. As Dad's body began to fade away, I felt a spiritual connection to him that continues to this day.

Taking on the responsibility of having a family member die at home is arduous and exhausting, but it can conjure up memories from long ago that have been forgotten but return with a tender poignancy. It is an opportunity for reconciliation and allows time to put earthly affairs in order. Watching a human body deteriorate is frightening, but the spirit shines forth as it prepares for new life.

There were times during the last twenty-nine days of my father's life that I was stretched to my limit, but I would have forever regretted the alternative. Because Dad had the courage to face his terminal illness and graciously accepted the help he needed to remain at home, Anne and I grew closer to our parents in ways that we never dreamed were possible.

CHAPTER 2

The Golden Years

"I'M FREE!" DAD EXCLAIMED. He was sixty-two-years-old and had just retired. "I don't gotta do nuthin!" He was exuberant. "I'll never wear a tie again," he said with a huge grin. The kids were grown and gone, the house was paid for, the dog had died, and it was time to hit the road. You would think a guy who traveled for most of his working life would like to stay put, but Dad wanted to get in the car and go. And after forty years of cooking, cleaning, and raising children, Mom was ready to eat in restaurants, sleep in hotels, and see the sights.

"Aw, how cute, matching car seat covers," I said. "You two are ready to go." I was happy for my mom and dad. They had met their obligation as parents, paid their bills and taxes, and now they were unencumbered. Dad was right—he was free.

For the next two years Mom and Dad left Ohio and drove through New England, the Upper Great Lakes, and Canada, stopping at war memorials and historic sites. Mom particularly loved the Civil War battlefields because she was a history buff. Dad liked to tour mansions in the Hudson River Valley and Newport Rhode Island, where the super-rich showed off their wealth in the eighteenth and nineteenth centuries. They went down south to Virginia, the Carolinas, Tennessee, and Epcot in Orlando. After a few years on the road, they began to consider leaving Ohio and moving west to be closer to Anne and me.

"I think Arizona is better," I told Anne. "The housing prices are much higher in California, and they have won't have enough money to buy an equivalent home. They want to move to a small town and live in a climate that has four seasons."

"I think Prescott would be good," Anne agreed. "It's a small town and has relatively mild winters. The snow melts quickly, and the summers aren't too hot. It's an hour and a half from Scottsdale. They need to live in the mountains to get four seasons."

Our parents bought a house on Hummingbird Lane in Prescott Valley, Arizona. The house had no basement, no lawn to mow, and was nestled against a small hillside that was dotted with evergreen trees. The kitchen window had a lovely view of the patio and the birch trees above it.

"I can't believe it, I really can't believe it. I'm in a new kitchen," Mom said as Anne and I helped her unpack dishes, pots and pans, and a myriad of kitchen gadgets. My parents were proud of themselves for making a cross-country move and were giddy as they settled in their new home. They had no regrets about leaving Ohio. While we arranged the kitchen, Dad was in the garage setting up his workshop.

"Your father isn't happy here, he wants to move again," Mom told me just six months after they settled into the house on Hummingbird Lane. "He can hear the cars on the highway at night, and it bothers him."

"Mom, you just made a huge move. That's a lot to ask." I was sympathetic. "I know," she sighed, "but he is determined."

Dad found a lot on Stony Ridge Road just outside of Prescott that was at the top of a ridge with a view of the valley below. He spent the next eighteen months supervising construction of the house. With sweeping views of the western sky, breathtaking sunsets and the snow-topped San Francisco peaks in the distance, the house was my parents' triumph over the flood-prone Ohio home where had they lived for thirty years.

"I'll take you on the tour." Dad couldn't wait to show off his masterpiece. "This is my workshop," he said. His table saw and drill press stood like sentries on either side of the spotless shop. The hand tools hung on a pegboard above his workbench. "Dad," I said, "this is a dream come true."

"Do you care to have an adult beverage?" Dad was proud of his fully stocked minibar. I sat next to the fireplace that rose from the hearth to the top of the two-story pitched roof in the living room. "Dad, your house is beautiful, congratulations," I said. I had never seen him so happy.

Then it was Mom's turn to show off her new kitchen. "Look at this big island. We can eat breakfast here. And let me show you the walk-in pantry. The deck right outside is where your father has his barbeque grill." My parents were like a couple of kids at Disneyland as they showed me their dream home. They moved in shortly before Christmas in 1986 and spent twelve happy years there.

Other than Mom's surgery in 1993, my parents enjoyed relatively good health. They had the southwestern United States to explore, so they went to Utah, Nevada, Oregon, and Washington. They drove to my house in Monrovia several times and stayed overnight. The next day I drove them to Long Beach so they could board a cruise to Alaska, Hawaii, and Mexico.

In the summer of 1998, the golden years came to an end. Mom and Dad stayed at Anne's house in Scottsdale while Dad underwent several diagnostic tests at the hospital. I called her that evening to find out the diagnosis.

"We are having a little moment here," Anne said when I called.

"What's going on?" I didn't understand.

"Dad's crying," Anne whispered into the phone. "The doctor told him he has colon cancer, and he's very upset and talking about his legacy."

"Dad's crying?" I was incredulous. "Call me later when we can talk."

No one had ever seen Dad cry. We Vallees don't cry. The only time I saw Mom cry was when she found out Dick got his girlfriend pregnant, but that was protest crying, not real crying. For a Vallee, real crying was an admission of weakness and just plain embarrassing.

The surgery took place the following week. The surgeon had scheduled another surgery before Dad's that took longer than expected. Dad was prepped and waiting in pre-op. The nurse said one of us could go back and sit with him, so I volunteered. He was lying on a very narrow gurney, low to the ground. I sat on a little stool next to him, and we talked about everything other than the fact that he was about to have eight inches of his colon removed.

"It's freezing in here," I said. "Are you warm enough?"

"I'm okay now," Dad said. "A nurse put these two blankets on me. She is a Buckeye too, from Columbus." Ohio's nickname is the Buckeye State.

"I guess the doctors like it cold so they'll stay awake during the surgery," I joked. He responded to my attempt at humor with a joke of his own. "Maybe the doctor made a mistake on the other guy and he's trying to cover it up," he said. We fended off fear with humor.

Dad was finally taken to surgery, and then Anne, Mom, and I headed for the surgical waiting room. The surgeon came out a few hours later and said he was pleased with the outcome of the procedure. "We got it all," the doctor said. "Mr. Vallee's prognosis is good."

We didn't know it then, but the colon cancer, despite the positive outcome of the surgery, was the end of Dad's healthy days. He was put on a regimen of chemotherapy that made him very ill. By Thanksgiving he had completed three months of treatment. Dad was too weak to drive to California for the holiday. With his physician's approval, my parents flew to the airport in Ontario, and I picked them up the day before Thanksgiving. The next day I was in the middle of preparing our Thanksgiving feast when Mom came down the stairs with a stricken look on her face.

"Your father is very sick." Mom's voice was shaky. "He has a temperature of 102 degrees."

"Mom, we've got to call Dad's doctor," I said as she dug through her purse to find the name and number of Dad's oncologist. The conversation was short.

"He said to take your father to the hospital emergency room immediately," Mom said. Several hours later, after he was admitted, we ate our Thanksgiving dinner out of Tupperware containers in Dad's hospital room.

The consulting oncologist who examined him the next morning asked Dad a question that none of us expected. "Mr. Vallee, why are you on chemotherapy?" She got a blank look from the three of us. She went on.

"With your type of cancer, at the stage it was at when the surgery took place, chemotherapy might have been optional," she said. We were stunned.

"You were probably part of the clinic's protocol," she explained. "Half the patients would receive chemo and the other half wouldn't. You could have chosen not to have chemo."

We were speechless. Then Dad spoke.

"I'm quitting chemo," he said. "I'm sick as a dog and feel like hell. I'm done." Dad was released from the hospital a few days later and never took another chemotherapy treatment.

My husband Paul and I drove Mom and Dad back to Prescott and got them settled in. Dad tried to resume his normal life, but never regained his strength and couldn't putter around in the yard or do woodworking projects in his workshop. Anne convinced Mom to hire a cleaning company once a week, but repairs and general maintenance stopped.

With Dad so weak and the two of them home alone most of the time, I worried. Mom didn't drive much after the move to Arizona. The steep roads in the mountain town of Prescott scared her, so she limited herself to trips to the grocery store, drug store, and the library. One day she pulled into the garage, didn't stop in time, and crashed the car into the back wall. She gave up driving altogether. Dad thought her garage mishap was funny. He didn't follow his wife's lead, and kept on driving.

Dad developed double vision just after Christmas. "I looked in the mirror and there were two of me," he said one day. We didn't know it then, but he was in the early stages of a condition called rotatory nystagmus, which would eventually rob him of his sight. His solution at that time was to put an eye patch on one eye and keep driving.

After several months off chemo, Dad felt well enough to take some day trips in the car. "We shouldn't have gone to Jerome," Mom told me confidentially when I visited them that summer. "Your father can't see well enough, and he drives too fast. I didn't look out the window, it was too scary."

"Mom! Why on Earth did you go to Jerome?" I asked, incredulous. "*I'm* scared to drive up that steep road. The hairpin curves are deadly." Jerome is an old copper mining town in Arizona that is 5,200 feet above sea level. Today it is a tourist attraction with a population of artists, craftsmen, writers and musicians.

"Your father gets cabin fever, and we like to get away from the house. But I don't think he's up to it anymore. His vision isn't good, but I can't say anything." My mother's ordinarily pleasant face was drawn with worry because we both knew there was no way to talk Dad out of driving.

Anne told me that a brand-new retirement community, Las Fuentes, was going to be built in Prescott. "We've got to get Mom and Dad to put down a deposit on an apartment," she said. "It would be a good place for them. I think Mom would like it."

"Dad won't, but he knows they are too isolated on Stony Ridge Road."

Anne agreed. "How can we convince them to move? They love their house. You are right, Dad won't want to live there."

We did what many adult children of aging parents do and gave it a hard sell. We double-teamed them.

"Mom, no more cooking or cleaning," I said. Mom's big smile gave us her answer, but neither of them wanted to put a $1,000 deposit down on a place that was still under construction.

"That's a lot of money to put down, Kathy," Mom said. They had enough money to pay for several cruises, but they balked at putting down a deposit to reserve an apartment at a retirement community. There were a lot of retirees in Prescott, and I worried that the new facility would fill up fast.

"We don't know if this house will sell right away; it needs some work," Dad said. "What if we change our minds? Is the deposit refundable?" I told him I'd find out. While I had a sense of urgency, they dragged their feet.

Leaving their dream home in Prescott was not only a loss of independence for my parents, it was an admission that they needed help, one of the great Vallee taboos. You never, ever ask for help. You do it yourself. Always. For Dad, moving to Las Fuentes was an admission of defeat. He called it "the home."

Before they left the house on Stony Ridge Road, Mom and Dad had a garage sale and sold belongings that defined them as autonomous—Dad's tools, the freezer, the vacuum cleaner. Most of their possessions had been accumulated over their fifty-six year marriage. They were literally putting a price tag on their life together. Dad laid out his tools on the driveway on a sunny Saturday morning and watched strangers walk away with them, off to unknown toolboxes, carrying away bits and pieces of his identity.

It was their last move, from a dream home to an apartment, from independence to group living, from enjoying their retirement to waiting for the next illness, one of which would end their lives. They were heartbroken; but in true Vallee style, they didn't complain.

The move to Arizona and the house on Stony Ridge Road were moves forward. Moving to Las Fuentes was a step back, toward dependence. The sadness I felt about my father's decline hung around me like the heavy winter coat I used to wear as a child in Ohio. Thinking of him as weak and vulnerable went against the grain. Watching my proud, self-sufficient father shrink before my eyes was a new kind of pain I'd never felt before. Pain usually passes, but I knew this one never would.

Six weeks after my parents moved into Las Fuentes, Dad had a stroke. He spent a week in the hospital and another week in the skilled nursing facility across the street from the retirement community.

Early one afternoon shortly after Dad was admitted, a nurse from the skilled nursing facility called Mom. "Your husband walked out of the facility, Mrs. Vallee," she said.

"The alarm sounded, so we were able to guide him back inside, but it would be good if you could visit and reassure him."

Mom and I walked over to the skilled nursing facility and saw Dad in the hallway, pushing a walker. When he saw us he lifted the front legs of the walker up and said, "Neighhh . . . neighhh . . . neighhh."

It was classic smart-aleck Dad, acting like he was riding a horse. In spite of myself, I laughed. Mom went as white as a sheet. Dad was released from the skilled nursing facility a few days later and went back to Las Fuentes.

The rotatory nystagmus caused Dad's eyeballs to move erratically, like Mexican jumping beans. He tried to lessen his symptoms by wearing a variety of glasses: his regular glasses, a pair he got at the 99 Cents Only store, and a pair of big block sunglasses. Nothing seemed to help, but when he wore the big blocks we didn't have to see his eyes do their eerie dance.

Dad started hallucinating after his stroke. Sometimes he saw a dog sitting by his chair, or he saw his mother. He'd sit in his Medicare lift chair and talk to her, or he'd say "Down, boy!" to an imaginary pup. Dad was under the care of an ophthalmologist for the rotatory nystagmus and had undergone a series of tests by his neurologist, Dr. Bryan, to try to pin down the cause of the hallucinations. "I'm falling apart," he was saying, more and more often.

One night Dad walked out of the apartment in the middle of the night, clad only in his pajamas and robe, and headed to the parking garage. The night security guard asked him where he was going.

"I'm going to get my car. It's in the garage," Dad said. "I have to go to work."

"Well, Mr. Vallee, it's a little early for work right now. How about you come back in the morning? What is your apartment number?" Dad told him and the guard escorted him back home. Anne installed an alarm that would buzz loudly when the front door was opened to alert Mom if Dad walked out of the apartment again.

"They moved to Las Fuentes just in time," Anne said when she called to tell me about the alarm. "I'm so glad there are people there to keep an eye on our wandering father."

"Yes! If they were still in their house, Dad could have gotten in his car and taken off to God-knows-where." I shuddered just to think about it. Our conversations were more and more often about how to protect our parents.

Role reversal is an easy concept to understand intellectually, but emotionally it feels like a shoe you can get your foot into but that just doesn't feel like it fits right. I never knew how much to do for Mom and Dad without embarrassing them or, worse yet, humiliating them. There was a lot of guesswork.

"Dad has an appointment with Dr. Bryan, the neurologist, on Friday," Anne told me during a phone call. "I don't think they understand what the doctor tells them. He has ordered tests, but when I ask Mom and Dad what the results were, they don't seem to know."

"Maybe I should go with them," I said. "I can come to Prescott on Thursday and go with them to the appointment on Friday. I don't think they'll mind." We were making plans for a party to celebrate Dad's eightieth birthday at Las Fuentes on Saturday, so it wasn't a problem to come one day early and see what the doctor had to say. "Great," Anne said. "I really want to know what Dr. Bryan has found with all the tests."

The neurologist's waiting room wasn't like a typical doctor's office. Little porcelain ducks with ribbons around their necks sat on the table with magazines, which were current. The fish tank was full of bright orange parrot cichlids, and the restroom could have been in a quaint country inn. But the charm wore off as we waited, and waited. One hour passed, and then we were shown to an exam room where we waited for another forty-five minutes.

"Does this guy always run so late?" I finally asked, failing to hide my impatience. I tried to be on my best behavior and not complain, but we were getting close to a two-hour wait.

"My butt hurts." Dad was getting grumpy too. Mom was annoyed but optimistic. "He'll be worth the wait, I'm sure," she said.

The windowless room was barely large enough for three chairs and the exam table. We stared at the door, willing it to open. Each squeak-squeak-squeak of nurses' shoes passing by raised our hopes that the door would open. At last, Dr. Bryan finally came in the room. He was tall and wiry, with close-cropped blond hair. A native of Texas, his slow drawl made him seem unhurried. He was likeable and unpretentious.

"Sorry for the long wait, Mr. and Mrs. Vallee," he said, drawling out the vowels. "We got a little behind today because of an emergency at the hospital. Is this your daughter? She looks just like you, Mr. Vallee, only a lot younger." We all smiled at Dr. Bryan's joke and forgot about the long wait.

He flipped through a thick chart as he rattled off a lot of medical jargon. The doctor was looking at the MRI and the EEG results, but when he said what they showed about Dad's brain, I didn't understand a word. No wonder my parents couldn't remember what he said. I was writing as fast as I could. He noticed, and slowed down.

The doctor stopped and read for a moment, then asked Dad how much he was drinking. He was concerned about the many medications Dad was taking and how they would react with alcohol.

"Mr. Vallee, my recommendation is that you drink one, two-ounce martini, twice a week." Dad had been a daily drinker for his entire adult life, and he simply couldn't process the information. Dad repeated back what he thought he heard the doctor say: "Two, four-ounce martinis, twice a day."

Dr. Bryan smiled and said, "That's one, two-ounce martini, twice a week." He emphasized, *one* drink, *twice* a week. Dad tried again. "Okay. Four, two-ounce martinis, twice a week." Dr. Bryan looked at me and I smiled. Dad was being a smart-ass. He was too old to become a tea totaler.

Dr. Bryan gave up. "Mr. Vallee, you don't drive right now, so drink responsibly." Although the discussion about martini consumption was more like banter than stern medical advice, Dr. Bryan wanted his patient to limit his alcohol consumption.

I couldn't understand most of what Dr. Bryan said, but it was clear that he found no evidence of cancer recurrence, which was a relief; but he still had no explanation for the hallucinations. Dad appreciated Dr. Bryan's good news, but there was something else on my father's mind.

"Doctor, my life is useless," Dad said. "I can't see very well, I can't drive, I can't see my computer screen anymore, and I can't watch TV."

"I understand, Mr. Vallee. It's got to be very hard. Have you participated in some of Las Fuentes' activities?"

"The old guys at the home complain about everything," Dad said. "They talk about how bad they feel, their aches and pains. That's all I hear." Dr. Bryan smiled when Dad called the upscale Las Fuentes retirement community "the home."

"Well, Mr. Vallee, I can understand your feelings," the doctor said. "Most people need a sense of purpose in their lives, and it's hard when they can't do what they used to enjoy."

That was the end of the conversation; what more could Dr. Bryan say? What could any of us say to Dad, who loved to be industrious and keep busy, when his life was so debilitated by illness?

I knew Dad was depressed about his limitations, but when he described them to the doctor, it was a punch to my gut. I realized how much he had lost. The guy who could fix a Chevy and install a gas-powered pump to get the water out of his basement every year during flood season was now dependent on others. The self-sufficiency so core to my father's identity was gone. Without saying it directly, Dad told his doctor he felt hopeless.

We went back Las Fuentes to have dinner. Mom went to the bedroom to change, and Dad and I were alone. Big-block sunglasses covered most of Dad's face, but I could tell by his body language he wanted to tell me something, and I became uneasy.

"I don't want to live like this anymore." There it was, flat out. My stomach lurched. Dad knew he wasn't going to get better, and there was nothing but illness and suffering ahead. He wanted to talk. I didn't. My heart was pounding, and my chest was beating like a bass drum. I was having a fight-or-flight response.

"I don't want to live like this. It's no good." Dad was expressing emotions that were not allowed in our family: fear, sadness, grief, vulnerability. He tried to fight them off, but they hit right between his eyes. The only feeling our family expressed was anger. That was the rule, and Dad was breaking it. Anger couldn't help him now. His feelings were laid out like those metal tools in the dentist's office.

I said something that acknowledged his feelings but offered no solution or comfort: "I know, Dad." I had no practice talking to my Dad in a soothing way. No one soothed or comforted Dad, not even Mom. When upset, he got mad and yelled; that was his release. He was trying to tell me how he felt, but this conversation was at a dead end. For a long time I couldn't think of anything to say.

"These past few years have been hard for you, Dad," I finally said. I didn't want him to live like this anymore either, but I didn't have the courage to discuss the alternative. If Dr. Bryan didn't know what to say to a man who was almost blind, in pain, and with a rapidly diminishing will to live, what could I say? One thing I knew: I could not tell him to buck up and fight. He had been fighting for the past two years, and his old age and illness had worn him down to the point that he could tell me that his life was no longer worth living. We weren't a family that suffered fools, and we didn't sugarcoat the truth. But at that moment I couldn't tell him the truth, because I had no words to express it.

Mom came bustling into the room, ready to go eat. I got a reprieve from my father's angst. I was relieved at the moment, but later regretted not saying more to Dad. I should have let him talk about his pain, his feelings. Our family taboo forbade expressing feelings like Dad had just done, and I wasn't able to break it.

Dad's birthday party was a great success. I brought his favorite cake from a bakery in Pasadena: chocolate with raspberry filling and lots of thick frosting around the edges. It had a big "Happy Birthday" in the middle. The Las Fuentes staff passed out slices of cake to the other residents. My husband Paul, a professional violinist, played duos with a pianist that included light classics and some old-fashioned sing-alongs that got everyone singing together. It was our last family celebration.

It was after Dad's eightieth birthday party, in July 2000, that Dr. Bryan ordered a more extensive MRI and got a diagnosis: non-Hodgkin's lymphoma. Early in August Dr. Bryan gave Dad the bad news. My father described it, in his own inimitable way. "When the doctor showed me into his living room (the doctor's office, not the exam room), I knew it was bad news."

Dr. Bryan told him that he had four weeks to live, without treatment. Dad opted for treatment, which was four weeks of radiation, followed by chemotherapy. He had enough fight left in him to try the radiation.

The bad news kept coming. "He sleeps most of the day, and he can barely walk. When he is awake, he stays in bed," Mom said. "He can't eat very well because the radiation treatments made his throat swell." These phone conversations went on for three weeks.

"That sounds awful, Mom," I said. "This is hard on you too. Do you eat in the dining room occasionally, to get out of the apartment?"

"No, I have dinner delivered," she said. "I don't want to leave your father alone." Dad ended his third week of radiation on August 25, 2000. Anne called me that afternoon. "I'm on my way to Prescott. They wouldn't do Dad's radiation treatment because his sodium levels were too low, and they took him to the hospital in an ambulance."

"What does sodium have to do with radiation?" I asked, not really expecting an answer.

"Mom said his throat is swollen and he can barely eat. The radiation is really hard on him," Anne said.

"This doesn't look good. How long can you stay?"

"At least for the weekend. I'll know more when I get there. I'll call you."

"I'll come next week," I said. As program manager for a nonprofit agency, I wore many hats. I went to my office that weekend and postponed some projects and left a list of tasks for my assistant to handle in the week ahead that couldn't wait. I left a message for my boss, who knew about Dad's illness. I wanted to get back to Prescott.

I kept replaying the conversation with Dad after our appointment with Dr. Bryan. I pictured him wearing the big block sunglasses and heard anguish in his voice when he told me he didn't want to live anymore. He worked up his courage to tell me, and when he did, I choked. I gave myself a pass for not knowing what to say when I was at the bottom of his avalanche of feelings, but I felt guilty that I didn't try to talk to him again. I didn't bring it up and never asked if he wanted to talk some more.

I wondered if he'd tell me again that he didn't want to live like this. I still didn't know what I could say to him, but I promised myself I'd do better, without having any idea what that might be.

Dad's family physician, Dr. Archer, told Anne that since Dad couldn't eat, a feeding tube could be inserted to deliver nourishment directly to his stomach so that the radiation treatments could continue. She got the message: In order to save him, we would torture him for as long as he gives consent.

"It's bad, really bad," Anne said when she called that evening. "Dad can hardly swallow, he's lost weight, and he looks like hell. Archer wants to put in a stomach tube so they can continue the radiation, but I don't see how Dad can take it."

"I'll be there on Sunday evening and we can talk," I said. "How is Mom?"

"She's glad I'm here, and she's driving me crazy," Anne said, sighing. "We're going back to Las Fuentes for dinner. Sis, I know Mom is under tremendous strain, but she keeps talking about when we kids were small children, telling the same stories over and over, and over again. It's like she wants to go back in time, when she was a young mother and her life was ahead of her. She doesn't want to acknowledge Dad's weakness, she doesn't want to contemplate her life without him." My sister was exhausted.

On Sunday evening I walked into Dad's hospital room in Prescott. Anne's shift was about to end at last. During the last few days she had dealt with doctors, coped with hospital routines, got more and more bad news and tried to keep Mom calm. She was relieved to pass the baton to me. It was my turn to run the next leg of this race that was becoming a marathon, with an uncertain outcome and no end in sight.

"Sis, you're here!" Anne exclaimed, as I walked into the room. Her fatigue was more than just lack of sleep. The stress had worn her out.

"Hi, Kathy," Mom said, "Thanks for coming." She didn't get up from her chair, so I went over and kissed her on the cheek.

"You two look tired," I said softly as I looked at Dad, who was asleep. They both nodded.

I sat down beside my father's hospital bed and looked at his emaciated body. He looked much worse than the last time I saw him. His face was gray underneath a stubbly beard, and his skin sagged. His lips were white with dryness. Anne had warned me there were lines on Dad's neck to direct the radiation. I imagined some faint lines from a felt tip pen, but they were thick and dark, and made his neck look like a target. He euphemistically called the radiation therapy his sunshine treatments, but the radiation caused the swelling in his throat that prevented him from eating.

I was glad his eyes were closed so I had time to adjust. As I looked at a man who was so clearly dying, I couldn't see the point of inserting a stomach tube to allow him to continue another week of treatment. We knew this would not save his life, or even prolong it much longer. After my initial shock, I felt tenderness, followed by determination and resolve to do better for him this time. He had taken a long shot with radiation treatments, and it nearly killed him. This was not how my Dad wanted to die. This time I would speak up; I would protect him.

Mom, Anne, and I knew Dad was dying, but we didn't say it to one another. It's not a conversation any of us knew how to start. Dr. Archer's answer was a stomach tube so that Dad could get more radiation treatments. Why would we subject him to more? More radiation was not the answer. We'd find another way.

Dad woke up when the nurse's aide rolled the dinner cart into the room. She raised the bed and supported Dad with some pillows. Then she moved the cart so the tray of food was in front of him. Three sections of the molded plastic tray held what appeared to be mashed potatoes, pureed peas and, everyone's favorite hospital dessert, green Jell-O. I thought of the times Dad put on his sports jacket and silver Navajo turquoise bolo tie and we drove to the Derby, our favorite steak restaurant, where he ordered a dry martini and a big, thick steak. We always ordered flaming baked Alaska for dessert. Memories of those meals fell down around me like leaves from a dying tree.

My father looked down at the tray and then at us. Giving his trademark grimace and wink, he bobbed his head as he tried to focus. Then he looked at the aide and said, "You want me to eat this?" The aide, a pretty young brunette who seemed unperturbed by Dad's dancing eyeballs, cheerily replied, "Yes, Mr. Vallee, I want you to eat this lovely food."

Dad managed to swallow some mashed potatoes and a few bites of pureed peas. Then he took a bite of the Jell-O, gasped, and began to choke. The nurse's aide leaned forward and lifted his shoulders. Dad pulled in air when he could, but it was mostly going out, trying to dislodge the Jell-O at the back of his throat. I thought Dad's lungs would fly out of his mouth. His eyes couldn't focus, but they could register fear. I went over to help the aide lift his shoulders, but it didn't help much.

I looked over at Anne and signaled silently, "This is really, really bad!" She signaled back, "Yup, really bad."

After fifteen very long minutes, the coughing slowly subsided. Dad waved the aide away when she offered him another spoonful. She pulled back. He'd had enough. The dinner cart was wheeled out of the room. A nurse came in to check Dad's catheter and help him brush his teeth. We took the opportunity to say good night.

As we left Dad's hospital room that evening, I was extremely worried about the next few weeks. During the last days of Dad's life, the fallout from the family feuds bore down full force, like the blizzards we remembered from our childhood in Ohio. Resentments piled up like giant drifts of snow, white and fluffy on top, but frozen solid underneath with misunderstandings, divided loyalty, jealousy, disappointment, feelings of rejection, and anger.

As the sun began to set, Anne drove out of the parking lot and headed back home to Scottsdale. Mom and I went back to Las Fuentes for dinner. The elegance of the dining room calmed both of us after our long day. The spacious, tastefully decorated room could have been in an upscale hotel.

Floor-to-ceiling windows provided a view of the small pond that was dug when the site was excavated. The pond was surrounded by small flowering trees, with a stand of cattails at one end. We sat next to the big window to watch the birds. Their tiny silhouettes bobbed and danced in the glow of the setting sun as they darted around.

We didn't talk much. With Dad's fate hanging over our heads, we each had our own thoughts. I broached the subject of the stomach tube.

"Mom, Anne and I talked, and we don't want the stomach tube because we don't think the radiation will cure Dad's cancer." She looked at me and grimly nodded in agreement.

"I'll call Dr. Archer in the morning and tell him there will be no stomach tube," I said. With that decision made, we parted for the evening. I eagerly returned to my hotel room. Mom and Dad had separate bedrooms in their apartment at Las Fuentes. Anne and I could have stayed in Dad's bedroom, but we both preferred a hotel.

The hotel was on the way out of town, out on the old highway. It sat on the top of a hill, with views of the valley below. I began to feel calmer as the car began the ascent up the long, winding driveway to the hotel and my respite.

I sat on the small balcony in my second-story room and watched the stars, so vivid in the dark western sky. I took deep breaths to expel the antiseptic smell of the hospital from my lungs. I couldn't as easily expel the uneasy thoughts I had about telling a physician that we didn't want to follow his medical advice.

We were Midwestern stoics. We kept our heads down and tried not to stand out. We avoided confrontation, too, especially with doctors. On that evening in August, I didn't know that the next day would be the hardest day of my life.

CHAPTER 3

It's Best When
the Family Decides

T HE NEXT MORNING I saw sunshine seep around the edge
of the blackout curtains, defeating the heavy drape's efforts
to stop its entry into the hotel room. I was filled with dread
and resented the sun's efforts to intrude on my dark mood.

I got up early so I could get to the hospital to see Dr. Archer
on his morning rounds. My parents had vowed to stay together
"until death do us part" more than half a century earlier. Now
that death was near, those words no longer seemed poetic. Just
like the sun, the past kept intruding as I focused on getting
through this day.

I couldn't find my car keys and glasses. Frustrated,
I stopped looking even though I couldn't leave the room

without them. I was officially discombobulated. My normal ability to organize my day was compromised by a cloud of unease. When I sat down on the bed to call Anne, I saw my glasses. Hopefully, my keys would appear just as magically.

"Hi, Sis, it's me," I said when she answered. "I need to talk to you about the stomach tube for Dad before I talk to Archer. What do you think?"

"The same as yesterday," Anne said.

"I'm going to try to talk to Dr. Archer on his morning rounds to tell him we don't want the stomach tube. If I can't, I'll call his office and see if I can talk to him." Anne wished me luck and said she'd stay by the phone all day. Our game plan was in place.

At the hospital I walked past the nurses' station and headed to Dad's room. Empty breakfast trays were stacked high, and wheelchairs, gurneys, and assorted diagnostic machines were lined up against the wall. The intercom beeped every few minutes followed by a request for a physician to "pick up line one." In this place of sickness and death, the disembodied voice of the intercom sounded like a chorus in a tragic opera, always in the background, plaintively requesting help, and occasionally reaching a crescendo by announcing a code. Patients hobbled along in skimpy hospital gowns, drab and wrinkled, backsides exposed.

"Your father just had breakfast," the nurse told me. "He still chokes a lot, but he got a little food down. He fell asleep right after he ate." Then she quickly left the room. Sleep was Dad's only relief from the choking, frustrating blindness, and the relentless boredom of the hospital. He slept noisily, with grunts, snorts, and some small gasps, but at least he could sleep. Dr. Archer was nowhere in sight.

I used the phone that was mounted on the guardrail of Dad's bed to call Dr. Archer's office. The receptionist put me through right away. When the doctor came on the line, I told him I was in Dad's hospital room and gave him a brief report about breakfast: that Dad managed to get some food down and was now asleep. Hearing Dr. Archer's voice made me feel as if I were about to walk out on a stage to deliver an unrehearsed performance. The orchestra was tuning, and I didn't have the score. Constricted throat, dry mouth, burning cheeks, ragged breath, sweating. I struggled to keep my composure.

"I talked to my sister and mother . . . our father is suffering with the radiation . . . he can't eat," I said.

I couldn't form a sentence, or take a breath. There was silence on the other end of the line. I tried again.

"Dad is suffering too much . . . we don't think the radiation will cure the cancer. He told me that he doesn't have a sense of purpose in his life . . . he doesn't want to live like this." I finally took a breath and my respiratory system kicked back in.

More silence. Dad let out a snort, and I turned away so he wouldn't hear me talk to his physician.

"Mr. Vallee is very ill. You can continue the radiation treatment, but he will need a stomach tube to give him nourishment," Dr. Archer said in a noncommittal tone of voice.

I took another breath and remembered Dad in his cotton robe, sitting in his Medicare lift chair, telling me that he didn't want to live like this. I had to tell Dr. Archer what Dad had said. I worked up all the courage I had left in my shaking body and said, "Dad told me he doesn't want to live like this anymore."

"I understand," his response was compassionate but reserved.

"We think it might be time for hospice." Finally, I said it.

"At this point, that is a good thing to consider. It is best when the family decides." His tone was suddenly lighter; he sounded relieved.

Dr. Archer had waited for me to say hospice. When I did, he immediately agreed. He said the family should decide, and we had decided. I was relived when Dr. Archer agreed that hospice was right for Dad, but right behind it, throwing punches, was fear.

"We need to talk to Dad about this. My mother, sister, and I have discussed it, but we haven't talked to Dad about the stomach tube or hospice. He'll want to talk about it with you, his doctor . . . a man."

Dr. Archer was surprised. "Doesn't your father know he's dying?"

Yes! I wanted to shout into the phone. *Yes! We know. Yes! Dad knows, but we need your help to talk about it with him.* I wondered why he let me stumble around the topic of Dad's imminent death when he knew his patient was terminal; but his immediate change to a positive tone of voice and his remark about it being best when the family decides gave me the answer. We had decided, but we needed to talk to Dad, and none of us were capable of having that conversation. We needed Dr. Archer to do it.

"Yes," I said, "we know, and Dad knows; but my Dad is quite traditional, and I think it would be easier for him if you talked to him, man-to-man. He needs to talk about this with a man."

Dr. Archer understood and agreed to help us talk to Dad. He suggested I call a few hospice agencies in town to get the process started. The conversation ended by his telling me that he would come to the hospital at 5:00 p.m. that afternoon.

I put the phone back in its cradle on the guardrail and willed myself not to cry. I'm not prone to weeping, but I knew that if I let my guard down, I would dissolve into big, racking sobs. I looked out the window with my back to Dad. It was a beautiful autumn morning, very sunny with a breeze rustling the leaves.

After the brief conversation with the doctor, our universe tilted. Dad was going to die. The certainty of his death sat flat in the middle of my stomach. Now that the word "hospice" had been spoken, Dad was released from his burden of trying to get better. I turned away from the window and looked at my father's sunken face and his thin, malnourished eighty-year-old body. I knew I had done the right thing, but it didn't comfort me.

I dreaded what was ahead. How would we get Dad from this hospital room to his home, where he could die in peace? How long would it take? Would he have pain? Could we take care of him? How would Mom cope? What if he choked and couldn't stop? My boss was sympathetic, but I ran a small department at my job and couldn't be away for long periods of time. There were too many questions and no answers.

As I walked out of Dad's hospital room that morning, I knew I couldn't quit in the middle of this job, a job that I didn't know how to do and would be considered well done when Dad was gone. A large part of Dad's work ethic was to always finish a job. "You never quit in the middle of a job," he'd say. "If you start a job, you finish it."

When I got on the elevator I remembered the last job Dad and I worked on together. It was many years ago, but a heavy fog of regret always rolled in when I recalled it. I chastised myself when I remembered what I put Dad through before I fully understood that he was old. I didn't realize it until we were in the middle of an awning demolition job that was too big for both of us.

Mom and Dad had come for a visit. I thought a demo job would be fun for Dad and me to tackle together, but my 1950s-style aluminum awning was too high above us and too heavy for my light-duty tools. We started on a hot summer morning, and by late afternoon the job wasn't close to being done. Tools were strewn about and stubborn slats still clung to the frame. Dad was clearly exhausted. His red face was pouring with sweat.

I looked at my dad and saw an old man. The realization was a shock. I had asked an old man to do a young man's job. I didn't understand that he no longer had the stamina to do heavy work.

"Dad, let's knock off for now, it's getting late and it's too hot. Let's finish tomorrow morning." He lowered his hammer and looked around at the big mess. He wiped his face with the sleeve of his polo shirt and looked at me.

"You can't quit in the middle of a job!" He was incredulous at my suggestion. At this rate, we wouldn't finish the job until midnight, but he was too proud to quit. Dad was still Dad, but he was old and tired, and we both knew we couldn't finish this job. I had made a huge mistake, and I didn't know what to do. I scrambled to think of a way for him to save face and to never, ever ask him to do a job like this again.

"Let's take the aluminum we have to the recycling center, and then use the money to buy drinks at the Derby," I said, hoping the mention of dinner at his favorite steak house would entice him to stop.

It worked. The image of a cool, dry martini and a big steak gave Dad an out, and he took it. He would have worked on that aluminum awning until it was totally demolished, no matter how tired he was. It was the ethic he lived by.

Now Dad was at the end of his life, and he needed my help. I wouldn't quit in the middle of this job. I would do everything in my power to provide my dad a safe passage home.

As I walked down the hospital corridor, the conversation with Dr. Archer played over and over in my head. When he said it was best when the family decides, he had no idea what kind of family we were. It was just the four of us, and none of us knew what we were doing.

CHAPTER 4

No More Do-It-Yourself

M OM WAS WAITING FOR ME at Las Fuentes, but I wanted to make the calls to the hospice agencies in the phone booth at the hospital before I went to pick her up. I didn't want her peering over my shoulder, interrupting, talking to me while I tried to carry on a conversation. I didn't have the patience for it. Big decisions had to be made, and the chief decision maker, Dad, wasn't going to be making them.

I was dipping a very large toe deep into the waters of Bob and Maryanne Vallee's power structure, and it was extremely uncomfortable. The conversation I just had with Dr. Archer marked a major shift in how things were going to be decided from then on. Although I knew Mom wouldn't have made the call, and was okay with me doing it, it felt like insubordination.

I had stood with my back to my father and talked to his doctor about ending his treatment.

Mom and Dad had stuck to themselves during their fifty-six-year marriage. Asking for help from anyone was unthinkable. Early in their marriage, after moving from Wisconsin to Ohio, they never asked members of their extended family for help. Mom was put on bed rest for the last six weeks of her pregnancy with John. Dad hired a woman to take care of the four of us—ages three, six, eight, and ten—while he was working out of town. Even under dire circumstances, it didn't occur to my parents to ask one of their relatives for help.

For Dad it was a point of pride to fix appliances, lawn mowers, cars, bikes, furniture, garbage disposals, and toilets. I don't ever remember seeing a repairman in our house. My parents' Midwestern stoicism was bulletproof. Asking for help showed weakness. Letting others into the family circle was an invasion of privacy. Even though there was no way my mother and I could have had that conversation without a medical professional's assessment of Dad's prognosis, I was still worried about how Mom and Dad would react. The more intense the problem, the more buttoned up they became.

Now our self-sufficient little clan needed help, and lots of it. Worst of all, we'd have to ask strangers for assistance. Mom and Dad had gotten this far by themselves, and they might tell me they'd get to the end in their own way. Since I had instigated this whole process, I would have to ask for help on their behalf, and then deal with the consequences.

There was a bank of old-fashioned phone booths in the hospital lobby, the wooden kind with a narrow seat. When I closed the door, a light came on. I looked in the Yellow

Pages under "hospice." There were only three agencies in town. I sighed deeply in the stuffy phone booth and dialed the first number.

The first agency asked for Dad's Social Security number before they asked his name. I scratched them off the list. The second one's recorded message assured me that my call was important to them. There was only one number left. I didn't know what I would do if they didn't work out. I had no Plan B.

"Hospice Family Care," a male voice answered.

"My dad is going into hospice, and his doctor suggested I call you," I said quickly.

"We can help you." His voice was reassuring. "What is your dad's name?" He wanted to know Dad's name. He was asking the right questions.

"Bob Vallee," I replied. His kind voice helped me relax, and I described our plight. "My dad is dying. I spoke to his physician a few minutes ago, and we are going to discuss hospice care with Dad this afternoon at 5:00 p.m." Then, in the privacy of the phone booth, I let the tears flow that I had kept in check all morning.

The hospice intake worker continued to ask me easy questions, which gave me a moment to compose myself. The overwhelming anxiety I felt during my conversation with Dr. Archer was gone, but in its place was sadness. I was talking about my father to a total stranger. I understood the enormous responsibility I now bore. The consequences of the decision to stop treatment landed squarely on my shoulders.

"Is your father in the hospital?" he asked.

"Yes." I didn't think he knew I was crying. I dug through my purse for a tissue.

"Where does he live?" he asked.

"At Las Fuentes Retirement Community." No tissue.

"Is he in Active Retirement or Assisted Living?" Good, another easy question.

"Active Retirement," I replied, somewhat boastfully. The residents in Active Retirement did not want to be associated with the more frail types in Assisted Living. Even in old age, there is a pecking order.

The intake worker was ready to set an appointment. "We can send a hospice nurse to see Mr. Vallee tomorrow morning at the hospital. Her name is Marlys, and she can come at 10:00 a.m."

"That sounds good, thanks." I wiped my eyes with the back of my hand and stepped out of the phone booth.

I was glad we were leaving the hospital, with its tunnel vision of cure at all costs, but I was scared of the new paradigm: letting the cancer take its course and allowing Dad to die with comfort care only. I was now acting like a parent or, more accurately, an advocate and caregiver. I needed to be sure of myself, but I wasn't. I walked out of the hospital that morning feeling far from sure of anything.

The two momentous telephone conversations ran through my mind. Dr. Archer was willing to have a very difficult conversation with Dad. The kind man from the hospice agency offered to help us care for him at home. I had asked for help, and the sun hadn't fallen out of the sky. In fact, it was shining brightly. I felt better, less alone, and my confidence increased. I hoped my parents would feel the same way.

During the short drive to Las Fuentes, my brain was in high gear. My heart was squeezed tight with dread and fear, but my head was composing a to-do list of all the tasks that had to be done. My head and heart competed for my attention. My heart sat at the top of the roller coaster, preparing to descend, while my head stood at the bottom, chastising me for not paying attention to the myriad details I'd have to manage. I knew the meeting with Dr. Archer at 5:00 p.m. would break my heart, and I would have to be strong. My head, the list-maker, would have to wait.

Mom and Dad's apartment was in the back of the facility, which was just as beautifully landscaped as the front. A desert sandstone retaining wall marked the perimeter of the property and was topped with evergreens and bottlebrush, their red spindly blossoms in bloom.

My parents were one of the first tenants and, in true Vallee style, had chosen the apartment at the back of the building. Their front door opened into an atrium with a large domed skylight that provided the area below with natural light. A fountain splashed water over several bronze statues of small children playing in a pool below and was surrounded by big pots of red and gold chrysanthemums. I paused for a moment to listen to the dancing water and look at the children captured in a moment of play under beams of sunlight that filtered through the glass roof above.

I remembered my seventh grade English teacher, Miss MacInthon. She made us memorize a poem once a month and recite it in front of the class. William Wordsworth's "Splendor in the Grass" came back to me in that atrium forty years after I recited it to my classmates.

> Though nothing can bring back the hour
> Of splendor in the grass, of glory in the flower,

> We will grieve not, rather find
> Strength in what remains behind,
> In the primal sympathy
> Which having been must ever be,
> In the soothing thoughts that spring
> Out of human suffering,
> In the faith that looks through death,
> In years that bring the philosophic mind.

I turned away from the fountain, comforted by Wordsworth's words, and rang the doorbell. Mom wasn't ready, so I sat in Dad's Medicare lift chair and waited. The TV was blaring. I put it on mute and picked up a magazine. The doorbell rang; I opened the door and was surprised to see a delivery person holding a floral arrangement of gold and orange fall flowers, accented with oak leaves and a spray of red huckleberry in a small wicker basket. I called out to Mom, and she came to see who sent them. She pulled the card from the envelope and read, "Dear Kathy and Mom: Thinking of you and praying for your courage and wisdom. Love, Anne." My emotions surged again, but this time they were positive. My sister was with me; we were in this together.

On the way to the hospital, we stopped at a used book-store to get Mom some paperback books. She loved historical fiction and just about any book set in England. She was an Anglophile whose favorite author was P. D. James. Then we went to the drugstore, filled both their prescriptions, and bought a couple of party-size bags of Hershey's Miniatures. We drove to Mimi's restaurant after that because we liked their soup and sandwich combo, and it was close to the hospital.

After we ordered our iced tea, I told Mom about my talk with Dr. Archer. "Mom," I began, "I talked to Dr. Archer on the phone this morning. When I said we were considering hospice, he said it's best when the family decides, but I told him we needed his help to talk to Dad. He's going to come to the hospital at 5:00 p.m." She didn't say anything, but nodded in agreement and paused for a moment.

"We need to tell your father that Dr. Archer is coming," she said.

"We'll tell him as soon as we get to the hospital," I agreed. The next topic was harder to discuss. I knew we had to start thinking about custodial home health care, which was expensive, and not covered by Medicare.

Dad would need help with toileting and grooming, and someone had to help him through his coughing fits. I had seen how the nurse's aides monitored him while he ate at the hospital. I didn't think he could eat by himself. The hospice nurse would visit twice a week, but Dad's day-to-day care needed to be provided by a home health aide. This was the proverbial rainy day my parents had saved for, and I knew they could afford to pay for it. After we ordered our sandwiches, I brought up the topic.

"Mom," I began, "I think you should have a home health aide in the apartment all day to help with Dad."

"No," she replied, "I can handle it." I soon learned that this would be her stock reply to all suggestions involving Dad's care.

"What will you do if he falls?" I asked.

"I'll pull the cord. The Las Fuentes staff will help me. They always come right away."

She had anticipated this discussion and was ready with an answer.

While the staff responded when the pull cords buzzed them in the office, Active Retirement residents were not permitted to use them too often. Mom had been pulling the cord frequently in the past few weeks, and the staff always came, but they would not come several times a day to provide personal care. Those were the rules.

"The cord is just for emergencies. You can't pull the cord every time Dad chokes or has to go to the bathroom." It felt as if I were trying to convince an exhausted toddler to take her nap. Since the idea of taking care of Dad wasn't resonating with her, I appealed to her self-interest.

"Las Fuentes has a prescription refill service," I said. "I talked to Valerie in Assisted Living about it, and she said they have an RN on staff who will monitor prescriptions for you and Dad and will make sure they are refilled. Best of all, an aide will deliver the meds to the apartment when you and Dad need to take them." I added, like I was a game show host and she had just won the grand prize, "You won't have to worry about a thing!"

She smiled at my attempt to sell her on something that she would not pay for and said, "I can handle it."

With each of my mother's negative responses, I grew more annoyed. I wondered how she could look at the weak and exhausted man who had taken care of her for fifty-six years and consider cutting corners on his care. But he had been in control from the beginning of their marriage, sometimes callously. She resented him and, despite my annoyance, I understood.

I dropped the topic, and we finished our sandwiches. As a peace offering I said, "Hey, let's order the chocolate mousse for dessert; we can split it." Mom smiled in agreement, and we shifted from heated discussion to mindless chatter, falling back on the way our family always dealt with conflict. We had a very tough afternoon ahead, and I didn't want to go into it with both of us angry. Although Mom and I couldn't agree on what would happen after Dad went home, we were united in our mission to talk to him about hospice and to do it as gently as possible.

As irritated as I was with Mom, I knew that our conversation with Dr. Archer and Dad would be the beginning of the end of Bob and Maryanne Vallee. I looked at my mother's tired face and hoped we could get through it.

CHAPTER 5

The Conversation

WHEN WE GOT TO THE HOSPITAL, Dad was coughing so loudly that Mom and I could hear him all the way down the hall. When we got to his room, he was shoving the wand of the suction machine to the back of his throat to clear out mucous. The "wand" was more like a device a plumber would use, but it did the job.

After the coughing subsided, Dad leaned back to rest. Mom walked to his side. That was unusual, because she usually headed to the chair in the corner when we entered the room. She walked toward him quickly and purposefully. He knew something was up.

The plastic under the sheets made a scrunching sound as Dad lifted himself up on his bony elbows. He struggled to get to eye level with Mom.

"Dr. Archer is coming at five o'clock to talk about hospice," she blurted out. This woman, who avoided expressing feelings, was disengaged from any kind of social life, and drank too much to stave off painful memories, had just stepped out of her comfort zone. It was the first time she had taken charge. I was impressed, and grateful.

I stood at the end of the bed and watched Dad's face as he looked up at Mom. His head wobbled on his scrawny neck. His parched lips were open, and his eyes, confused and frightened, made him look like a hatchling. I hoped he could withstand the conversation we were going to have with Dr. Archer.

"The radiation isn't working, and your throat is so swollen you can't eat. We don't want to put a feeding tube in your stomach. I can't stand watching you suffer anymore; you've suffered enough." Mom summed it up. She gave him permission to leave her, to give up the fight. She let him know before Dr. Archer came.

Mom kept her hand on Dad's arm. He looked at me. I didn't say anything but nodded my head. We didn't tell Dad we loved him; the taboo against saying such words was not breached. Nonetheless, there was profound love in that room, expressed in our own way.

"Dad," I said, "you've fought hard, and you've suffered a lot to get well. The radiation isn't going to beat the cancer."

"Archer is coming?" he asked.

"Yes," I answered, "He'll help us."

I moved from the end of the bed, stood next to Mom, and put my hand on his arm, next to her hand. We stopped talking. Dad launched into a full-blown choking fit. Mom moved back and I lifted his shoulder. I hit the button to elevate the bed and stood next to him until the choking subsided. He grabbed the suction wand and waved me away. I sat down.

Dr. Archer walked into the room at precisely 5:00 p.m., nodded to Mom and me, and went to Dad's side. He was tall and thin, with gray at his temples, worry lines in his forehead, and tired, kind eyes. He was empty handed: no chart, prescription pad, white coat, or stethoscope. He got right to it.

"How are you feeling, Mr. Vallee?" he asked.

"Lousy," Dad answered, eyes wiggling and jumping. No matter how weak and tired he was, Dad did his best to maintain a dignified bearing. He had a light cotton robe on over the hospital gown. The wisps of his hair weren't combed back in the usual style. Dad tried to keep his manner calm and reserved in spite of his rumpled appearance.

"The radiation has been rough on you," Dr. Archer said.

Dad drew his skinny legs up under the white sheet, as if gathering strength to continue the conversation.

"I feel like hell," Dad said.

"Hell" was a constant reference in my father's life. He loved to tell the story about the time he told one of his high school teachers to go to hell in the middle of class and got expelled. On hot summer days in Ohio, when the humidity and the temperature was in the high nineties, he'd say, "It's hotter than hell." Now his whole life was hell. He wanted out.

Dr. Archer leaned closer and gave it to him straight. "Mr. Vallee, a guy like you . . . in your condition . . . we consider to be terminal."

I was frozen in place.

Dad gave a little hiccup, the same precursor to crying that I'd inherited. He pulled the sheet higher, and I thought he might pull it over his face. He squeezed his eyes shut and dropped his head back. Dr. Archer took a step closer and put his hand on Dad's shoulder.

"Can we try the chemo?" Dad asked, in a soft, plaintive voice. I felt my heart break like bone china hitting a concrete floor. As sick as he was, Dad still thought he might get better. I watched the last bit of hope drain out of him. I had to pull it together. I couldn't collapse now.

Dr. Archer kept his hand on Dad's shoulder and replied. "If you take the chemo, you'll feel even worse than you do right now. You'll feel sicker." He emphasized *worse,* and *sicker,* as he described how Dad would react to more treatment. Dad shook his head and said, "I don't want to feel worse. I can't get any sicker."

Dr. Archer paused for a few moments. Dad sat quietly, his head slightly bowed. The doctor was waiting to see if his patient needed to talk some more. He stood silently and watched Dad closely. There was no need for Mom or me to say anything.

Dr. Archer's compassionate guidance got us through a life-changing moment. He was a highly trained physician, but it wasn't his medical knowledge that came through; it was his humanity. He was honest with Dad about his chances for recovery, but he spoke with kindness. Mom and I needed to be there to support Dad, but we never could have had this conversation without the doctor.

Dr. Archer began to discuss how the Medicare hospice benefit would work and the services it would provide. We all felt the shift in focus, gently guided by Dr. Archer. The awful moment had passed, and we were on a new road, one that would take us away from the hospital, the oncology clinic, and the intensive care unit. It was time to go home.

I didn't know it then, but that excruciatingly painful moment with Dr. Archer and Dad was the reckoning that had to happen for us to get to a place of acceptance. Dad's courage at that moment, when his hope was taken away, and the grace with which he accepted the inevitable, helped sustain us during the following twenty-nine days, the last days of his life.

"I want to get the hell out of here," Dad growled. His voice was raspy, but strong and certain.

Dr. Archer said Dad could leave as soon as arrangements were made with the hospice agency for him to receive care. There would be no more painful treatment, no more ambulance rides to the hospital, no more false hope.

Dad told Dr. Archer he had had a good, long life. He looked at Mom, and then at me. We nodded in agreement. Dr. Archer smiled and nodded too. Dad took the diagnosis the doctor had given him with great strength. His first response to his imminent demise was gratitude. What a classy guy.

"Thank you, Doctor," he said. Dad lifted his hand towards his physician for a handshake. Dr. Archer responded by holding his patient's hand with both of his. "You're welcome, Mr. Vallee."

We were all relieved. Dr. Archer's skilled guidance helped direct us to hospice. There was one thing I knew for sure: Dr. Archer had given my Dad the information in exactly the way Dad wanted it—straight up—man-to-man.

Dr. Archer looked at me and nodded, as if to indicate that all was well and began to walk out of the room. Now that this difficult task was done, he seemed anxious to leave.

It was getting late. Dinner had been held because the doctor was in the room. Dad was tired and hungry and knew he faced a battle to get his food down. Before we left, I told him a hospice nurse would come to see us at 10:00 a.m. tomorrow. He looked startled for a moment and then realized that I had set the appointment before the conversation with Dr. Archer. He didn't seem to be mad at me; but he had just had the most difficult conversation of his life, and getting upset with me wasn't high on his priority list.

Mom and I went back to Las Fuentes for dinner. We got settled at our favorite table by the window and gave the young waiter our order. After he went to get our iced tea, Mom and I talked about what had just happened.

"I was pretty surprised when Dr. Archer told Dad he considered guys like him terminal," I said.

"Me too. Dr. Archer knew the right thing to say. He knew how to talk to your father." The waiter put two glasses of iced tea on our table.

"We couldn't have said those things to Dad," I said. "It had to come from the doctor."

"We needed Archer. He did a good job," Mom agreed. "The radiation made him so sick that he stayed in bed all day, and now he can't even eat. This isn't the way he wants to live."

"Once Dad understood what Archer was saying, he felt he could just let it all go." That is what I thought, based on Dad's response to the doctor. "It was so hard to see Dad like that. I wonder what he's thinking about now, all alone at the hospital." We both started to tear up, so I changed the topic.

"When I came to Prescott for Dad's seventieth birthday, you two had just gotten back from a trip, and he was putting the suitcases back in the storage closet," I said. "Out of the blue Dad said he was going to live another ten years and then he was going to croak. He was in good health then, so it must have been a pretty easy thing to say."

"That sounds like your father," Mom said, with a tired smile.

"I told him not to talk like that," I said. "It isn't good karma to predict when you will die."

"Here we are, six weeks after your father's eightieth birthday," Mom said as she shook her head. "I wish he hadn't said that."

The waiter brought our plates to the table. We had both ordered meatloaf with brown gravy and mashed potatoes, comfort food tonight. I slathered the dinner roll with butter while Mom and I talked about Dad and his fate.

"Mom, do you remember that story Dad told us about when he got the horse serum and almost died? He said he got a glimpse of the other side and he wasn't afraid; he was content," I said.

"Yes, he talked about it a few times," Mom said. "It was 1938 and he was only eighteen. No one knew he was allergic, so the family doctor gave him horse serum, and all of the sudden he couldn't breathe. Grandpa rushed him to the hospital. Your dad was lying on a gurney in the emergency room when he grasped Grandpa's hand and said 'Bye, Dad.' Every time he told that story he always said he wasn't afraid because the other side was peaceful." We were quiet for a minute.

I saw a piece of chocolate cake and a slice of cherry pie on the dessert cart and said, "I'm going to have a piece of cake. Are you ready for some pie, Mom?"

"Of course. I'll have cherry pie," Mom said. In spite of our exhaustion, we dug in to our desserts.

As I walked Mom back to her apartment, I worried. We had been through a profound experience together and were still coming to terms with it. I didn't want to leave her alone. Mom struggled to get the key in the lock when we returned to the apartment.

"Mom, are you going to be okay by yourself?" I asked.

"I'll be fine, don't worry," she said. "See you tomorrow morning." We were a family of introverts who craved quiet time alone.

As I drove back to the hotel, I looked at the dark sky in the high desert town. Incredibly vivid stars seemed within reach. A shooting star cast its light across the sky just as I reached the crest of the hill.

I didn't go to my room right away but sat outside by the pool. I hoped to see another shooting star but none appeared. The pool was cool and aquamarine, lit by underwater lights. Three lively evergreen trees danced in the late summer breeze.

I took several deep breaths, trying to exhale the antiseptic hospital air out of my lungs. I tried not to think of anything, not of the day behind me, or the day ahead of me. I had brought a glass of wine to the pool. Before I took a sip, I held the glass up to the sky and delivered my favorite toast.

L'chaim . . . to life.

CHAPTER 6

The Phone Calls

I WAS IN CHARGE OF A large mannequin. It was wooden and moved stiffly. There was a problem with its eye, so I cut it with a knife, but cut too deeply, and half its eye fell off and floated into space. Its mouth fell open. I screamed.

My scream jolted me awake. My heart was pounding, and my hair was soaked with sweat. The stress of the past few days had fed my unconscious with ghastly images. I pulled my wet hair back and tried to untangle myself from the damp sheets. It was 2:30 a.m.

I got out of bed and went out to the small patio. The cold air hit me like a slap in the face. The light desert breeze lifted the heat from my scalp, and my damp pajamas grew cooler. I tried to shake off the awful images from my dream before I went back inside. After a few minutes I started to feel chilly, so I went back to bed and slept through the rest of the night with no more frightening dreams.

When my alarm went off at 6:00 a.m., I got out of bed quickly, took a shower, and got dressed. I had to get a lot done in a short amount of time. There was no margin for error. The meeting with the hospice nurse had to go well. Dad's future was in my hands. I was tense, but I hoped the meeting this morning would be easier than the one with Dr. Archer last evening.

I replayed the conversation with Dr. Archer over and over in my head. The look on Dad's face when the doctor said guys like him were terminal was seared into my memory. The meeting with Dr. Archer altered the course of my parents' life. I was scared and unsure of what was ahead, but kept moving forward.

I opened the blackout curtains, and the brilliant Arizona sun flooded the room like a tsunami. I sank back into the pillows on my bed and drank tea while I talked to my husband Paul on the phone. It was refreshing to talk about everyday things, unrelated to disease and death. I was ready to face another momentous day.

Mom and I had breakfast in the dining room at Las Fuentes. I enjoyed talking to the young waiters, who were unfailingly polite and cheerful. I thought about the hungry pack of five kids Mom had fed every morning before she had her own breakfast. Now it was her turn to sit and wait for breakfast in the elegant dining room.

"You look tired, Kathy," Mom said.

"Gee, thanks, Mom." I joked. "Okay, I confess, I was at the Yavapai Casino last night and lost track of time. Lady Luck was not kind to me. I'm broke."

"I can loan you a few bucks for gas," Mom quipped. We both laughed and made eye contact like we used to when we talked about easy things, when no one's life was at stake. It felt good.

As we made the short drive to the hospital, I started to talk about what Dad would need when he came home. I had already mentioned the prescription service which Mom nixed, but it was worth a try again now that Dad was in hospice.

"Mom, I'm really worried about Dad getting his meds," I began. "He's got to have the Decadron four times a day because it keeps his brain from swelling. What will you do if he needs pain medication? What if he chokes?" I tried to keep my voice from sounding accusatory. We were both tense.

Mom didn't bother with her usual response, "I can handle it." She took a new approach. "I'm not paying for home health aides," she declared. "It's too much money."

"Mom," I said, "you can afford it, and you will pay for it." I was getting so angry I considered ending the discussion, but decisions had to be made soon. Neither Anne nor I were signers on their checking account. Mom would have to pay the bills.

"You have never spent one day or one cent taking care of an elderly relative. You didn't take care of your two aunts who raised you after your mother died. Your brothers and their wives did. You need to take care of Dad, and you need to do it right." I was digging up ancient history and it wasn't fair.

"My brother Jack told me I didn't have to take care of our aunts because I had so many kids. I don't have to take care of your father. I have you and Anne to do that." She was needling me. I took the bait that she laid so neatly at my feet. I knew I was walking into a trap, but I couldn't stop myself.

"Let me get this straight . . . because your brothers took care of your aunts, then you think you don't have to take care of your husband?" I said, resisting the urge to lean over and push her out of the car.

"Yes, that's right," she declared.

As I parked the car in the hospital parking lot, I realized there was nothing left to say for now, but I knew I had a battle on my hands.

We got to Dad's room one hour before the appointment with the hospice nurse. Dad was on the phone. I wondered who was on the other end. Dad wasn't saying much, just nodding and saying short phrases like, "It's good to be prosperous" and "That sounds good."

It had to be my brother Dick, the king of one-sided conversations, and it was obvious he was talking about himself. Anne had left messages on Dick, Jean, and John's voice mail about the stomach tube and our decision to enter hospice the previous evening.

After our conversation last night with Dr. Archer, I felt close to my parents in a way I had never experienced before. I cherished the new relationship we had forged together, on the knife edge of grief, sharpened by excruciating pain. But at that moment I snapped right back into our childhood pecking order where Dick was at the top and the rest of us ran a distant second.

Memories flooded over me: Dick shorting me on the profits when we shoveled snow off the neighbor's driveway, of getting the wind knocked out of me when I fell off my bike while we were soaping windows on Halloween and him calling me a baby. Hauling sheep manure up a ladder from the basement to the crawl space for his failed mushroom farm.

Dick called his father once he knew that death was near, and not a moment sooner. Dad was happy to hear from him, but I resented his sudden appearance at the eleventh hour. After twelve years of virtual silence, except for a present sent to Mom (nothing for Dad) at Christmas, I wondered what Dick had to say.

This was not the time to get knotted up in family grievances, a task as hopeless as untangling Christmas tree lights.

After he hung up, Dad looked at us, visibly shaken, and said, "That was Dick. Jean called too." Mom asked what they had to say, but Dad didn't answer. He was too shocked to speak. I'd never seen him so distraught. His emaciated body shivered like a skeleton performing a macabre dance. He coughed a little before he spoke. I was afraid he would start to choke, but he didn't.

"Jean said she regretted the estrangement," he said in a soft, hoarse voice. She had called earlier that morning. "Dick said his rental properties are doing well."

Dad put his hands up to his face and began to cry. He kept his hands over his eyes and tried to talk, but his swollen throat was further constricted by emotion, and he could not form the words.

My broken heart, still in a shambles from the last few days, was ready to burst with a blistering rage at my two siblings who didn't return Anne's phone calls when Mom was near death after her surgery seven years earlier and when Dad had colon cancer two years ago. Heartbreak is quiet, but outrage is loud. I felt both at the same time.

"It's good that they called," Mom said. "It's good." Dad looked at her and nodded. This was their moment. I moved towards the door to leave the room.

I ran down the hall to the pediatric wing of the hospital and called Anne from the phone booth.

"What the hell? They both called? Double whammy for Dad, that's for sure," she said.

"Yup, both called. Dick bragged about his business, but I don't know what Jean said."

"Bastards." My sister fueled my outrage. It felt good.

"What a couple of jerks." Venting helped me calm down.

"Call me if you need to talk," Anne said.

"Bye. I will." I appreciated her offer. I was as calm as I was going to get, so I headed back to Dad's room.

The wrenching experience with Dr. Archer had changed me. I felt fiercely protective of these two people who had put their trust in me, and I didn't want to let them down. We'd made a compact, set our course, and were focused on a very uncertain future. None of us wanted to rehash the past; it was too painful. The wisdom of the old cliché, "What's done is done," applied to our family. The hospice nurse would be here any minute, and we were about to see how she would help us get Dad home.

CHAPTER 7

The Rest of Your Life

SHORTLY AFTER 10:00 A.M. a woman strode into the room and walked to the end of Dad's bed. She was a tall, middle-aged brunette, tastefully dressed in a blue plaid skirt and cream-colored sweater. She had the natural confidence that nurses have and looked as if she had had a lot of experience with this kind of meeting.

"Hello, Mr. Vallee, I'm Marlys, from Hospice Family Care. I spoke to Dr. Archer this morning, and I'm here to talk to you about hospice care," she said, looking only at Dad. Dr. Archer must have told her about Dad's impaired vision because she stood where he had the best chance of seeing her. Then she looked at me.

"I'm Kathleen, Mr. Vallee's daughter, and this is my mother, Mrs. Vallee," I said, grateful that she called Dad "Mr.

Vallee" and not "Bob." We were off to a proper and polite start. She asked if she could sit down. Dad nodded and she sat on a chair next to his bed. I felt as if my parents and I were in a lifeboat, being hoisted up the side of a big rescue ship.

"Mr. Vallee, I am here to talk with you about the rest of your life. You are entering a new phase in your life. Hospice care will provide you, and your family, the support you need to make it the best quality it can be." Marlys swept us up in her positive attitude. She was talking about the quality of Dad's life, not the end of it. She lit up the drab little hospital room. Our fairy godmother had arrived and was waving magic dust over us. My family's isolated world was about to change. To me, it felt good. I wasn't so sure about my parents.

"I want to get the hell out of the hospital," Dad said.

"Certainly, I understand," Marlys replied. "Dr. Archer said you live in the Active Retirement wing at Las Fuentes. Do you plan to go back there?"

The three of us said, in unison, "Yes."

"Good, that is an excellent facility. Are you going to have help at home?" she asked.

"Yes," I answered before Mom could say anything. "We are going to have home health aides."

"Have you interviewed them yet?" Marlys asked.

"No," I replied. "My sister Anne is getting some numbers for me to call."

"They'll probably want to come to the hospital to meet Mr. and Mrs. Vallee before setting up the schedule," she said.

"I'll call them as soon as I can," I assured her. Mom leaned forward, as if to speak. I gave her a look, and she sat back, clutching her purse with both hands.

Marlys began to list the tasks I would need to complete before we took Dad home. Now that Dad was enrolled in hospice he would be discharged from the hospital as soon as preparations for his care at home were completed. The custodial care must be in place, the medical equipment ready, and the prescriptions filled. I hoped to be ready by the end of the day and take Dad home on Wednesday.

Although Mom was listening to Marlys, the hospice nurse knew I would be the one who would get everything done. I wrote as fast as I could on my legal pad.

I had bought the pad, a clipboard, and a ten-pack of pens at the drugstore the day before. I put pens everywhere: the car, the hospital room, Mom and Dad's apartment, the hotel. I couldn't eliminate my anxiety, but I could compensate by overstocking pens. At this point, I did whatever worked.

The legal pad became a part of our caregiving team. Anne and I passed it like relay runners pass a baton. We kept Social Security numbers, doctors' phone numbers, errands that had to be completed and instructions on how to make Dad's martinis on the legal pad. It was an annex to our over-stressed brains, and we depended on it.

Marlys explained that Medicare would pay for all medically necessary drugs and medical equipment. "I've got to have this," Dad said, and pointed to the suction machine that was mounted on the wall.

Marlys assured him that portable suction units could be rented from the medical equipment store. She gave me some numbers to call and told me the equipment had to be in the apartment before Dad could go home. I had to reserve a Medi-Cab to take him home from the hospital. The to-do list was getting long. I began to wonder how I'd get it all done in one day.

Marlys paused and asked if there were any questions. Dad waved his hand, indicating that he had one, but first he coughed a few times to clear his throat. We waited.

"Did anyone ever go into hospice and not croak?" Dad asked.

My heart crashed, just like it had yesterday when Dad asked Dr. Archer if he could try the chemo. He wanted to pull off a miracle, be the one-in-a-million.

"Yes," Marlys said, "there are miracles. Although it is rare, it does happen."

That was Dad's only question, so Marlys turned to leave. She handed me her card. "Call me anytime," she said, reassuringly. "If I'm not in the office, they will page me." I took the card and shoved it securely under the clip at the top of my clipboard. After Marlys left, I got Mom settled with her paperbacks—two were by P. D. James, so I knew she'd be content—and began my errands.

I entered Las Fuentes through the Assisted Living wing. Valerie, the receptionist, smiled at me. Phones, intercoms, and clipboards were not in sight, and the area looked more like the front desk of an upscale hotel than housing for the old and infirm.

"How is Mr. Vallee?" Valerie asked.

"Not too good," I replied. I knew we'd have to tell people at Las Fuentes that Dad was in hospice, but I wasn't ready just yet, so I asked to talk to Karina, the staff RN who administered the prescription service. Valerie showed me to Karina's office and asked me to sit down.

"How is your Dad doing?" Karina asked. She was very young but had an air of confidence and empathy.

"He is in the hospice program. It was a very hard decision to make, but we feel it is right for Dad. I want to make the next few weeks as easy on my parents as possible, so I am going to enroll them in the prescription refill service. My sister and I won't be with them all the time, so I want to make sure they both get their meds, especially Dad," I said.

"We have found that the prescription service is good for our residents in hospice. Having an aide come into their apartment to give them their meds on a regular basis is reassuring and will also let us know how your parents are doing," she explained.

"That's what we need," I said. "I'd like to sign the paperwork now. Dad will be coming home tomorrow." The bill for the service would be included in the rent, so Mom wouldn't have to write a check. Big relief.

"Please let us know if there is anything else we can do," Karina offered.

"Thanks, I will," I said as I left her office.

I started down the hall to my parents' apartment. When I got there the door was open because the cleaning crew was there, so I headed to the kitchen and went directly to the cupboard where Mom and Dad kept their prescriptions.

I called Anne. She picked up on the first ring. "I'm in Mom and Dad's apartment," I said. "I just signed them up for the prescription refill service. The cost will be applied to the rent."

"Good." Anne was relieved. "What meds do they have in the apartment?"

"Let's see. Baby aspirin, Lipitor, Decadron, and two bags Hershey's kisses," I said. "There are some empty bottles here too. Marlys said we have to throw out all medications and start fresh now that Dad is in hospice. Karina and Marlys will coordinate with the pharmacy."

"This would be very hard to manage on their own," Anne said. I agreed, and I told her I would keep her posted and hung up.

I sat for a moment in my parents' apartment and looked at the things they had accumulated over the past half-century. The one-hundred-year-old Gustav Becker chiming clock from Grandma and Grandpa's house was on the mantle, along with Mom's collection of Hummel figurines. On the round table between their two easy chairs was a huge gaudy lamp that had to be fifty years old. I teased them about the big behemoth, but they liked it, so it stayed. I looked at the huge Western prints by Ted Blaylock that Dad collected with scenes of Old West towns nestled in the mountains. My favorite was one of a grandpa walking with his small grandson along a path above a snow-covered village.

I felt the essence of my parents in the room. They had spent most of their lives together. They were content with one another and had enjoyed the years they spent in Arizona. Soon Mom would be alone, and I worried about how she'd manage. I felt nostalgic for my childhood and a deep melancholy for my parents.

Before I left, I used the phone in the apartment to call the front desk and asked the maintenance department to remove Dad's bed and put it in the storage room in the basement of the facility. They assured me they would do it right away.

As I was driving to the medical equipment store, Anne called and gave me the number of a home health agency she liked. It was owned by a married couple. They charged $9.50 per hour during the day and $10.50 at night. That seemed reasonable to Anne and me, but probably wouldn't be to our parents.

Dad wouldn't pay a guy to put chains on his tires in the snowy Prescott winters. When I was a kid, I watched him try to fix the dishwasher himself, and he almost got electrocuted. He painted his own house, trimmed his own trees, and took care of his family. Now he couldn't do any of that. I would have to find a way to convince him to get help from other people, but I had no idea how. He wouldn't want to pay someone to take care of him; he would consider it a waste of money.

My parents pinched pennies while they raised five children. After they retired, they traveled a lot, but they were still frugal in their day-to-day life. They didn't hire a cleaning service or a gardener, they didn't eat at extravagant restaurants, and most of their trips were to National Parks and Epcot. They would consider the idea of paying for personal care in their home to be too expensive and way too intrusive. It would be a hard sell.

I ordered a suction machine, oxygen concentrator, hospital bed, transfer bench, and commode from the medical equipment store. Their deliveries were done for the day, but they assured me they would deliver it all tomorrow, no later than 5:00 p.m.

I needed to call Dr. Archer's office to see when he would discharge Dad from the hospital. It was already late in the afternoon, and I didn't know when the medical equipment would be delivered or if the maintenance department had removed Dad's bed. I hadn't interviewed home health aides. I wasn't ready.

As I drove to the hospital, I realized that while my plans were in motion, I couldn't put them in place in one day. Medicare would no longer cover the hospital charges now that Dad was in the hospice program. Time was short. This myriad of details was stressful, but it took my mind off what would happen when Dad got home.

When I walked into Dad's hospital room, Dr. Archer was there. I was relieved, because I needed to tell him that I wasn't ready to take Dad home on Wednesday. I explained to the doctor that my plans were in process, but not yet completed. Dad looked disappointed. I assured both of them that Dad would be ready to go home Thursday morning.

"Well, I see you are working on it. I think Medicare can pay for one more day," Dr. Archer said. Now I had a fairy godfather who was as wonderful as my fairy godmother. I felt my body relax. Another day was all I needed, and the good doctor gave it to me.

"We can get out of here on Thursday morning, I promise," I said to Dad. "I have to be sure we can take care of you at home." As I ticked off all the tasks I had started, but had not yet completed, he looked at me like a kid who wanted to leave camp early. I knew how much he hated the hospital.

Mom and I went back to Las Fuentes and had a glass of wine in the apartment before dinner. When we got to the dining room, we had a pleasant conversation, like normal people who weren't about to bring someone home to die. I didn't talk about money, and she didn't mention how good it was that Dick called. After two incredibly intense days together, we were mellowed by the wine and got a little goofy.

Mom was staring out the window, with her head propped up by her hands. The pond was lit at night and created a charming scene, with the stand of cattails by the edge of the pond casting a bristly shadow.

"Do you remember that summer when we went to Michigan for a vacation and your dad rented a camper?" Mom asked. I started laughing. That trip was a disaster.

"That was the most miserable trip we ever took!" I said, laughing harder. "Dick and Anne had summer jobs, so it was just you, Dad, Jean, John, and me. The little camper was too small for us. The mosquitos were brutal; we had welts the size of saucers. Dad got the flu and stayed in the camper all day." Mom was grinning at me.

Jean got a fishhook in her ear, and Dad had to drag himself out of bed to take her to the emergency room. The so-called bathroom in the camper was a joke, and we had to use the communal showers in the campground," Mom laughed. "We couldn't wait to leave!" We were getting a little loud, but we didn't care.

"That was the worst part," I said. "It was a gang shower, right out of a prison movie." We were now laughing so hard tears came to our eyes. Recalling that terrible vacation released our tension.

"I was glad we took that trip," Mom said with a twinkle in her eye.

"What? Why?" I was incredulous.

"That trip killed any ideas your dad had to use a camper for us to travel in after we retired." Mom had a satisfied look on her face.

"So that miserable trip guaranteed you would stay in comfortable hotels instead of a crummy little camper," I said. Mom nodded, with a big smile. We ended our meal together, still chuckling. I left Mom at the door to her apartment with both of us still cracking jokes about our vacation from hell, and I headed back to the hotel.

When I got back I sat by the pool. The humorous reprieve was over. My anxiety returned. I welcomed the solitude and hoped to find some peace of mind before I went to my room. A gentle breeze rustled the trees, but I didn't relax. Instead, I kept seeing my dad, weak and vulnerable, struggling to maintain his dignity and composure, as he sustained one crushing blow after the other. I was bone tired and emotionally depleted.

In the midst of my despair, I began to feel a subtle shift in mood. Some words of the Twenty-Third Psalm came to me. *Yea, though I walk through the valley of the shadow of death, I will fear no evil/ for Thou art with me. Thy rod and Thy staff, they comfort me.*

I loved that psalm because the words gave comfort and solace. The first few lines, with visions of green pastures, and still waters, had always calmed me. The valley of the shadow of death was a powerful image, a frightening metaphor. We were, quite literally, in the valley of the shadow of death. I didn't understand how a rod and a staff, ancient tools of shepherds, could comfort me.

As the words of the psalm sifted through my mind, the breeze stirred. The scent of cedar wafted over me, and then through me. My spirit rose up, as gentle as a feather, as true as first love, as clear as a summer sunrise. And then I knew: Thou art with me.

I had asked for help, and it had been freely given. Dr. Archer, hospice nurse Marlys, RN Karina, the staff at Las Fuentes, and our soon-to-be hired home health aides had become my rod and my staff. They were with me, and they would comfort me.

CHAPTER 8

Tantrums and Tenderness

W HEN I GOT TO MY PARENTS' apartment the next
morning, Dad's bed was gone. I thought I'd be
relieved, but childhood memories rose up unexpectedly, and
I felt forlorn. My focus had been on meeting Dad's medical
needs, so I didn't expect such a strong emotional reaction
when I saw the big gap in the room where his bed used to
be. My parents' bedroom furniture was a constant in my own
life, as well as Dad's. I felt like a little girl again, looking in
my parents' bedroom, knowing that I wasn't allowed to go in.

Shortly after they got married, my parents bought a complete bedroom suite with a double bed, two bedside tables, a
tall chest of drawers and a dresser. Made of maple, the varnish
gave the wood a luminous sheen. It was the only bit of elegance
in our home in Ohio.

The master bedroom wasn't much bigger than the kids' bedrooms in our no-frills ranch-style house. The floor was dark green linoleum, dotted with little white flecks. The walls were a light shade of green, and the curtains (not drapes) were beige. The bed was covered with a floral cotton bedspread, topped with two pillows. It wasn't cozy or inviting, but to me, the room looked very fancy. I longed to go in, but I wasn't allowed. It was a kid-free zone.

We kids never got in bed with Mom and Dad on Sunday morning. Occasionally, I'd race in and stand by Mom's side when I had a particularly scary nightmare, but she took me back to my own room to calm me down. Mom and Dad never welcomed their children into the safety and comfort of their bed. It was theirs alone, and now it was gone.

I called the front desk, thanked them for moving the bed, and reminded them to let the medical equipment delivery men into the apartment. I was anxious about the row of dominoes I had lined up. Every piece would have to fall into place, or my plan would fall apart. If Dad got home and the hospital bed weren't there, I didn't know what I'd do. He had to have the suction machine, the oxygen, all of it.

Mom and I got to the hospital just before 9:00 a.m. Walking into Dad's room was different that morning. My parents and I had cleared the painful hurdles to prepare to leave the hospital and were looking forward to Dad's homecoming. None of us had doubts, or second thoughts. Dad was going to die in his own way, on his own terms, in his own home. My parents and I were in new territory, and we were scared and uncertain, but we were steady in our resolve. There was no going back.

Dad was awake and had eaten breakfast. He was choking less and eating more. I was surprised at how much the swelling had gone down in just a few days. His color was better, and his mood was chipper because he was going home. No matter what was ahead, it had to be better than the last three weeks. My father was counting on me, a fact that made me proud one minute and terrified the next. I was on an emotional seesaw and couldn't find a steady balance point.

Patti, a capable-looking woman in her mid-forties, with auburn hair and a kind smile, walked into the room and introduced herself. She and her husband, Tom, owned Helping Hands, a home health care agency. She handed me her brochure and explained what services they provided. We listened intently.

"Our caregivers are bonded and thoroughly investigated," Patti said, to establish her credibility and the reliability of her staff. "They will help you with bathing, eating, toileting—what we call custodial care."

Dad coughed and cleared his throat. "I just need help in the morning and at night." Mom nodded. Patti said she could schedule a caregiver for two hours in the morning and two hours at night. I knew that wasn't enough, but kept my mouth shut.

"How much is it?" Dad asked. I held my breath.

"The rate is $9.50 an hour," Patti said. *That's cheap,* I said to myself, *only $38.00 a day.* It was hard to keep still, but I needed to stay out of this.

Dad looked in Mom's direction and she nodded. He hated having strangers in his home, but he knew he would need help when he left the hospital. My parents didn't invite friends into their apartment, much less strangers. They didn't host the poker game, they didn't have friends over to watch football games, they didn't throw parties for each other's birthdays. They were loners who liked their privacy and were happy with each other and the TV. This would be a huge adjustment.

"When would you like to start?" Patti asked.

I couldn't keep quiet any longer and said, "How about tomorrow night?"

"I'll check the schedule and get back to you right away," Patti said. I was writing the details on the clipboard when Patti handed me her card. I secured it under the clip. Mom and Dad seemed satisfied with the arrangement, so after Patti left, I excused myself and called Anne.

"Is that all they'll agree to?" she asked.

"Yes, it isn't enough, but I hope they'll get used to it and want more help."

"You sound tired," Anne said. "How are you holding up?"

"Getting through the conversation with Dr. Archer was the hardest thing I've ever done. Then Dad asked the hospice nurse for a miracle. Dick and Jean topped it off by calling out of the blue, but I'm still standing."

"Have some chocolate today, lots of chocolate." My sister knew me well.

Mom and I walked to the hospital cafeteria for lunch. After we'd taken our trays to the table, I told Mom that Anne and I thought she and Dad should have the aides for more than four hours a day.

"Oh, no, Kathy, that's too much money." Tiny bits of cottage cheese dotted her tongue. She couldn't take a moment to swallow before she vetoed my suggestion. As she gulped down another spoonful, I could see Mom was doing the math in her head. If the charge for four hours of care were $38, then the charge for twenty-four hours would be more than $244. Dad was three weeks into the four-week life span he was given. He wouldn't need the care for long; we had a short horizon.

Mom had bought the groceries, cooked the meals, and cleaned the house for the past fifty-six years. She had been on duty twenty-four hours a day, 365 days a year for the first twenty-five years of her marriage. Our family never ate at a restaurant or ordered a pizza. Dad cooked only when Mom was too sick to get out of bed, which was rarely.

She lugged the laundry for seven people down the basement steps, then washed, dried, and ironed it (in the days before permanent press). Then she lugged it back up the steps again. Mom wasn't going to pay another woman to do domestic work now.

"Mom, custodial care is a whole new ballgame. Can you see yourself changing Dad's diaper, or emptying his suction machine? Do you think you can stand next to him while he pees to make sure he doesn't fall?"

She gave me a blank look, paused, and said, "I can handle it."

I tried to control my temper. Getting mad at Mom just shut her down. She was being asked to pay people to take care of her husband, and she wasn't having it. Dad couldn't dominate her anymore. Now that she could make decisions independently, she felt free to say "no."

We left the cafeteria with Mom adamantly refusing to pay for more than four hours of care a day. We went back to Dad's room and sat together while he slept. I needed to escape. I told Mom I had to make some calls and went to the pay phone in the lobby.

I called home, and my twenty-four-year-old son Ben answered. The sound of his voice made me homesick for California. I missed my family. I wanted to sleep in my own bed and not have terrible dreams. I wanted to go to dinner and a movie with my husband. I even wanted to go back to my job.

I told Ben how frustrated I was with Grandma and how I wanted to hire help for Grandpa but that she wouldn't agree. He listened for a while and then said, "Mom, do you remember when I was three years old and had temper tantrums?"

"Yes!" I remembered it like it was yesterday. Ben would throw himself on the floor and writhe around in circles, kicking and screaming, protesting the injustice of not getting his way, especially in the grocery store when he knew people were looking.

"Just treat Grandma like that," my grown son said. "She is having a temper tantrum. Do what you have to do."

Ben was right. He had sized up the situation and given me good advice. I knew two things: My parents needed help at home, and they could afford it. There was no guarantee that home health aides would smooth the path for Dad, but I knew that without them, my parents would lurch from crisis to crisis, and Dad would be the one to suffer. Role reversal was easier with Dad. With Mom, I'd have to take a different approach. I thanked my astute son and hung up.

I sat in the little phone booth and considered my options. Then I did what I had to do. I pulled Patti's card from the clip on the clipboard and called her. When she answered, I told her we wanted home health aides twenty-four hours a day, seven days a week. She told me she could arrange it, and the first aide would come at 6:00 pm on Thursday evening. She reminded me that the hourly rate was $10.50 from 6:00 p.m. to 6:00 a.m. It was a small price to pay for having a home health aide throughout the night.

Then I called Anne. "I just talked to Patti and asked her to schedule round-the-clock coverage. We know Mom and Dad won't be able to manage by themselves, and we can't let them find that out when they are in the middle of a disaster."

"That's good, Sis. It's better to have more care than not enough. Mom and Dad can afford this; it's their rainy day." With confirmation from my sister and son, I left the phone booth, much lighter on my feet.

The oppressive sense of uncertainty and fear I had been carrying around for the past three days was beginning to lift. The meds were set up, Dad's room was ready for the medical equipment, and, most important, the home health aides were scheduled. Dad had a safe place to die with dignity. I feared his actual death less than the dying process. I couldn't prevent his death, but I could protect and comfort him in his final days.

I went to Dad's room to get Mom. We said good night and headed back to Las Fuentes. Mom and I were congenial, mainly because I stopped talking about hiring help for Dad. I didn't tell her about my phone call to Patti. She would find out once Dad was settled and my plan was in place. We stopped at the bank of mailboxes before we went to the dining room. Mom showed me a letter from John, addressed to Dad.

We both knew it was John's farewell to his father. Dinner in the dining room was our only quiet time of the day, our respite. We really needed it this evening, and now this bittersweet bombshell landed in our laps.

"I can't read this," Mom said. The look on her face made me want to cry.

"I know," I replied. "Let's have dinner and then I'll read it to you." Mom nodded in agreement.

During dinner we speculated about what John had written. Neither of us thought it would be unkind or full of recrimination. John wasn't that kind of guy. Mom had her cherry pie, I had my chocolate cake, and then I opened the envelope. Enclosed were three typewritten pages. I began reading.

> *Dear Dad:*
>
> *We should say these things more often, and sooner. It's too bad it has come to this, but we're Vallees and we don't show ourselves to each other very often.*
>
> *The last time I talked to you, you told me that you admired me. I want you to know that meant more to me than anything you've said to me in the last 43 years. (I know I'm 44, but I had some difficulty with the English language that first year.)*
>
> *I admire you, Dad. You've done a lot and accomplished a lot in your long life, and you have some pretty impressive things to show for it; not the least of which are five fine children.*

Overwhelmed by my brother's tenderness, I had to stop reading, to collect myself. His thoughts were simply stated, but powerful. When he wrote that we Vallees don't show ourselves to each other very often, he meant never. This was a first. His opening three paragraphs broke down the walls of inhibition. In the next part of the letter John described Dad's career and his retirement years in Arizona.

You called yourself a peddler, but Mom called you a Manufacturer's Representative. From the beginning of your career, you wanted to be independent, so you formed your own sales company and worked on straight commission. We kids knew that you sold many things: tools, table saws, drill presses, go-karts, folding ladders, saw blades, camping tents . . . the list goes on and on. We watched you get on the road every Monday morning, on your way to make sales calls in Ohio, Indiana, and Michigan. Although I was only a kid, I knew you were an honest man, with integrity. When you took samples home for us to use, you always paid for them. We really loved the go-karts.

By the 1970s the economy tanked and you lost your major accounts. I know that was hard on you, Dad. Money was very tight. You gave up the independence that was core to your identity, and took a job with a salary—and a boss. I learned from you that a man does what he has to do to support his family.

In 1984 you and Mom sold the house in Ohio, pulled up stakes, and moved to Arizona. You settled in Prescott and built a beautiful big house on the top of a peak. Best of all, your workshop was built on daylight grade, no longer in the basement, with room for everything.

By then your reflexes weren't what they used to be and your days of operating power tools were over. The workshop sat, unused, for several years. It had to be tough to sell your house and your fifty-year collection of tools and move to a retirement home.

I stopped reading for a moment and looked at Mom. John was with us; we felt his presence so deeply that we didn't need words to acknowledge it. His loving tribute was a balm for us, a soft goose-down comforter that wrapped us in pleasant memories.

We were both awash in tears, but we weren't self-conscious or embarrassed. John had broken a big family taboo—expressing feelings of love. The power of his words, written so plainly, but expressed so elegantly, released us from our inhibitions.

I began reading again. John shared an intimate memory of Dad and him that squeezed our hearts, pushing out more tears. John had a congenitally deformed left hand, with stubs for fingers, but a full thumb. My parents never allowed him to limit himself because of it. John watched Dad cope with his own deformed right hand, which was claw-like, his fingers immobile, from an injury he sustained at age nineteen in a farming accident.

There are some memories of you that will always live on. I remember the time we were both working on the lawn mower downstairs in the workshop. Normally that stuff took place in the garage, but this was a tough one and we got it closer to where the tools were. We had the engine completely torn apart and were reassembling it, trying to get the breaker points put back together. You picked up a small screw and dropped it. Then I picked up the screw and dropped it too. You looked at me and said, "kinda tough having a bum mitt, huh?" I guess we shared that too, but I got mine the easy way. I learned because that is all I had. You knew the difference.

I stopped because my voice seized up and my throat closed. Mom and I were back in Ohio, in the basement, watching a father and son fix a mower. We could smell the musky air and feel the chill of the block walls and the cement floor. We saw Dad and John working under fluorescent lights, struggling with a mutual disability, but never once giving up.

I looked at Mom to see how she was doing. I saw pools of emotion in her eyes that I had never seen before. We were having a moment with John, but we were also having a moment together. We had struggled with one another in the past few days, but John's words softened us, opened us, and brought us close. I felt as if I were holding a bubble in my hand: shimmering, fragile, and incredibly beautiful. There was one more page. I slowed down and let my emotions surface, as we Vallees rarely do.

I learned self-reliance from you, Dad. I always admired the way you would fix something just by taking it apart to see how it worked and then getting all the pieces put back together again. I admired how you could take a couple of sheets of plywood and turn them into nightstands or cabinets. One of my earliest memories is playing with my friends in the basement, and we were talking about what our dads did for a living. I remember saying that "my dad was a Wood Man." You didn't sell stuff, you made things out of wood!

Dad, you did what you thought was best and tried to instill honor and integrity in your kids. You gave me creative drive and showed me that I could do things for myself. You showed me by action and deed that there was nothing that couldn't be fixed, anything can be figured out. It is satisfying to do things yourself. I'm passing that legacy on to my kids. I know they'll use it well.

I know showing emotion is tough for you, Dad. There were so many things I wanted to tell you when we visited, but we've never done that before. I never truly appreciated everything you'd done for me until I had my own two sons. Our children always imitate us—the good and the bad stuff. But seeing them imitate the good stuff is rewarding. I hope you saw the good stuff in me. I love you, Dad,

Your youngest,
John

"Mom, this is a beautiful letter. Dad will love it, but I'll have to find someone to read it to him because it is too hard for us." Mom nodded in agreement. In the next few days I did find the perfect person to read John's letter to Dad, in the place we least expected to find him.

I walked Mom back to her apartment and made sure she put the letter in a safe place so it wouldn't get lost. John's heartfelt words gave both of us a poignant ending to another challenging day. As we said good night, it was a comfort to know that Dad would get a loving tribute from his youngest child.

CHAPTER 9

Home

ON THE WAY TO THE HOSPITAL Thursday morning, I worried about how I would take care of Dad. I remembered the old cliché about how hard it is to do the "right thing." So easy to say, but not so much when you are staring down the "right thing's" barrel.

Dad was asleep when I got to his room. I stood by his bed for a few minutes and thought about John's letter. After I read it to Mom last night, I had a different perspective on Dad's impending death. John's reflections on his childhood memories had been intimate and moving. I had been so focused on the present, I hadn't thought about my own memories of Dad when I was a child.

Early on a Sunday morning when I was about ten, Mom and Dad were sleeping in while we kids watched TV and ate our Kellogg's Frosted Flakes. I decided to make a bongo drum out of a round Quaker Oats container. The knife slipped, and I cut my hand in the space between my index finger and thumb. It hit the fleshy part in the area that was stretched tight like a hammock as I gripped the container. I pulled my hand back and was horrified to see that I could look through the small cut in my skin and see my muscles inside.

I let out a piercing scream. "Moooom! I hurt myself!" There was no blood gushing, but the small wound terrified me. I ran from the kitchen, tore through the living room, and threw the door to my parent's bedroom open. I was afraid of entering their sanctuary, but this was a life-or-death emergency.

"I cut myself! I'm huuuurt!" I was in full panic mode and had my parents' undivided attention.

"Kathy, calm down and let me see," Mom said, trying to assess my injury. I held out my hand, and she flinched a little but stayed calm and told Dad she thought I needed stich. A stitch? I'd never had a stitch. I would have to go to the doctor, and he'd probably give me a shot. I started to cry again.

"I'll take her," Dad said. Take me where? If Dad was going to be in charge, this was serious business.

"Kathy, stop crying. Dad is going to take you to the emergency room so a doctor can look at your cut. Go get dressed. Did you eat breakfast?" Mom's soft voice calmed me down.

"I ate breakfast already. I wanted to make a bongo drum out of the Quaker Oats carton, but the knife slipped and I cut myself," I sobbed. Mom and Dad looked at each other, obviously relieved that I hadn't done more harm to myself, but slightly amused by my bongo drum project.

It felt strange to be alone with Dad in the car. In a family as large as ours, it was rare for one of our parents to go somewhere with just one of the kids. I sat in the front seat and held the washcloth Mom gave me on my wound.

"We are going to the emergency room at the hospital," Dad said. Not only was he not yelling at me, he was pretty mellow.

"Am I going to get a shot?" I asked.

"Maybe," Dad said. "When you get a cut they usually give you a tetanus shot. I've had one."

I felt like crying again, but I was sitting in the car with my dad, going to the hospital. I decided to be brave. I held back my tears all the way to the emergency room at Blanchard Valley Hospital. I walked through the automatic doors next to Dad, expecting the worst, but grateful that he was calm and gentle. He sat with me while I got a shot and one small stitch.

I smiled at that memory as I watched Dad sleep. Then I remembered May 4, 1970. Dad drove across the state to rescue me from Ohio University after Governor Jim Rhodes shut down all state college campuses in response to the killing of four students at Kent State. We were given twenty-four hours to leave.

Things had been tense for several days at OU. Student demonstrators were becoming violent, and rumors flew around campus. I stayed put in my dorm as tension mounted. After the shooting, National Guardsmen came to the OU campus and stood in the streets with their M-16 rifles extended, standing silently.

"Your dad is in Cleveland. He's coming to get you." Mom managed to get a call through to the pay phone at the end of the hallway in my dorm.

"Mom, Cleveland is far away," I said. "I have to get out of here."

"He'll be there as soon as he can. He's on his way," Mom said. I got all my things crammed into a few boxes and walked across the village green to return a library book at Alden Library. The smell of tear gas wafted through the air and stung my nostrils as I hurried back to my dorm.

"Let's get out of here," Dad said. He had driven past the guardsmen and was visibly shaken. We loaded the car and left quickly. I slept almost all the way home.

Those memories of Dad were from my childhood and young adulthood, but most of my memories of my parents were when they were older, after they retired. My own children were grown. Mom and Dad invited my husband Paul and me to join them on short car trips, never lasting more than three days, which was our family's limit for time spent together.

On our trip to the North Rim of the Grand Canyon in 1994, Ben came with us, but didn't stay in the cabin with the old folks. He took his tent and backpack and headed to the campground. In the middle of happy hour, a mouse ran across the room in our cabin, and Mom didn't scream. I was shocked.

"Mom, you always screamed your head off when you saw a mouse in the basement back in Ohio," I said. "I learned from you to scream when I saw a mouse."

"I guess I'm over it," she said, casually sipping her Manhattan. "We have lizards in Arizona, and I think they're kind of cute." I was too proud to say that I was still squeamish about mice and woke up several times that night, convinced the little critters were in my bed.

Our next trip, in 1996, was to Solvang, a small Danish village in the Santa Ynez Valley in California. We were in Dad's big Oldsmobile, with him at the wheel, Mom in the front passenger seat, and Paul and me in the back seat. Suddenly Dad got into an altercation with another driver, also an old guy. Mom, Paul, and I hadn't seen what happened, but Dad was mad. He opened the car door and started yelling at the other motorist. The old guy opened his car door, too, and the two men started mouthing off. The other guy punctuated his anger with obscenities.

"Screw you!" the old guy screamed.

"Bob, get back in the car," Mom whispered in a trembling voice.

"Dad, get in the car now," I urged. "You don't know if the guy is armed."

"Bob, you really need to get back in the car right now," Paul said quietly.

Dad responded to the male voice and got back in the car. His last words to the other old guy were almost endearing.

"Do you think you should use that language in front of your wife?" was Dad's parting shot to his enemy.

I dusted off more memories. This one took place when Paul and I visited Mom and Dad just after they moved into the house on Stony Ridge Road. It was a lovely summer evening, with a cool mountain breeze sifting through the dry Arizona air. My husband and I sat in the spacious living room and watched the weathered mountains fade from azure blue to steel gray until the sky was dark enough and the stars shone bright. The conversation was light; we were full of great food and wine, enjoying our leisure.

Dad brought out a bottle of cognac. He told us his dad had given it to him more than fifty years earlier. He had saved the French brandy all this time, waiting for the right moment to share it, and that moment was with Paul and me. He carefully poured the cognac, and as I took the stemmed glass, delicately etched with roses, I knew Dad expressed his love for me in the way he knew how.

I didn't realize how long I had been standing there by Dad's bed, lost in memories. I needed to stop thinking of the past and get ready for this momentous day.

"Dad, it's me, Kathy," I shook his shoulder gently as I spoke. His eyelids lifted and his eyeballs were jumping and jiggling. He was startled and tried to make eye contact, but he couldn't see. I kept talking, hoping he would recognize my voice.

"Dad, the Medi-Cab will be here at 11:00 a.m., and we can get out of here," I said. He finally realized who I was and said he wanted breakfast. Now that he could eat, he was always hungry.

"Where is your mother?" he asked.

"At home," I told him. "She is going to put out the American flag." It was the only job I could think of to provide Mom with an excuse not to go to the hospital with me.

He seemed to be okay with that and gave his affirmative grimace and wink. I wanted to take him home without any "help" from Mom. Maybe he knew that, maybe not. Mom was always Dad's second-in-command. Now I had inserted myself into this duo as a sort of deputy. At this moment, it worked.

When I took Dad's shirt and pants out of the closet, I realized how much weight he'd lost. The pants were going to hang on him. Luckily, suspenders were attached. Dad cared a lot about how he looked and always dressed well. My grandparents' photo album was full of pictures of an elegant family with two handsome sons in three-piece suits, hair slicked back in the style of the day. There was an eight-by-ten-inch photograph of their Great Dane, Major, sitting at attention on the perfectly groomed lawn.

Now I was about to dress my dad in a pair of big pants, old-man suspenders, and dirty socks. I started with his shirt. He was like a toddler, flailing his arms around inside as I pulled it over his head. I recognized it as the blue polo shirt I had given him for Father's Day. I helped him into his baggy pants and got the suspenders over his bony shoulders. I pulled his crusty socks over his feet. I chastised myself for not bringing clean clothes. Dirty socks were not Dad's style.

"I feel like a little kid," he muttered sheepishly. As I helped him with these simple tasks, I was glad I had hired home health aides. It would be easier for Dad to be helped by a stranger than by me or Mom. I felt more confident about getting twenty-four hour care. One minute I was doing a good job; the next, I forgot to bring clean clothes.

"You probably helped me put my socks on a few times," I replied, knowing it wasn't true. Mom always changed our diapers, dressed us, potty trained us, and put a sweater on us when it was cold. Mom wanted to write a book entitled *Fifty Thousand Diapers*. That was ten thousand diapers per child for five children. Dad didn't change one of them. He may never have put my socks on, but he did what husbands and fathers did in the 1950s: He provided a home for us and paid the bills. Now I was helping him in the best way I knew how.

Putting those socks on seemed like a privilege to me, as my father leaned up against the bed, putting his skinny foot out to meet my hands.

"Where is my toiletry case?" Dad said. I found it in the small closet and handed it to him.

"Hey, Dad, this is the one you had when you were working," I said as I handed him the well-worn case. The brown leather toiletry case was at least forty years old. Dad got it from ThermoServ, a company he sold insulated pitchers and cups for, when he exceeded his sales goal. The inscription on the inside was still visible: "You are up, so sell something."

"They wanted to remind you to work, even before you brushed your teeth," I said.

"I liked it better after I retired and didn't have to sell a damn thing anymore," Dad replied.

"You got that right," I said, remembering all the times I saw the toiletry case on the bathroom sink as Dad got ready to head out for a week of work on the road. He took it on his retirement travels to savor his leisure.

"Where is my comb?" Dad said as he dug through the case. We both knew that his toiletry case, so essential for most of his adult life, was now obsolete. This would be the last time Dad would search through his toiletry case, looking for his comb, or shaver, or blood pressure pills. Loss hit me like those raindrops that hit the ground so hard they bounce back up, and then hit the ground again.

"Here it is," Dad said and ran the comb through his thin hair, combing it straight back as he had for the past eighty years. Then he ran his electric shaver over his chin. My father had prided himself on being well groomed during his adult life, but no comb or shaver could conceal his gray skin and the dark circles under his eyes. The blue lines on his neck from the radiation were still visible above his shirt collar. He gave the grimace and wink. He was ready.

"You look good, Dad," I said brightly, trying not to cry.

"I look like hell," Dad replied. "I just want to get out of here."

"When you get home you can change into clean clothes. You'll sleep better there. It's noisy in the hospital and it smells too," I said. Dad nodded in agreement.

"I'm hungry." Dad wanted breakfast. Just then a nurse's aide walked through the door and put the tray on the bedside table. Dad carefully spooned small bits of oatmeal into his mouth. It was lumpy and watery, but he managed to get it down. After a few moments the aide was satisfied that I could monitor him and left the room.

"The food will be better at home," he said. He'd given up on the oatmeal and was eating scrambled eggs.

"You've always liked the food at Las Fuentes," I agreed. "They'll cut it up so you don't choke. I think we'll be home in time for lunch so you can try it out."

Hospice nurse Marlys came with some bad news. "The Medi-Cab won't be here till 2:00 p.m. I ordered it for Wednesday morning, and you stayed another day. Unfortunately they are very busy today." It was my fault because I didn't tell Marlys Dad was staying another day. Chalk up another demerit.

Dad and I groaned in unison. We had worked so hard to be ready on time. "We'll wait here," I told Marlys. Dad was too weak to wait much longer. I was worried because he looked like he might fall over at any moment. He had been admitted to the hospital in a severely depleted condition and had only gotten weaker in the past four days. I needed to get him out of the hospital as soon as possible.

Marlys knew what bad shape Dad was in. I looked at her with pleading eyes while Dad lay back in the bed. "I'll see what I can do," she said as she walked out the door.

A moment later Dr. Archer walked in, clipboard in hand, with Dad's release papers. "Mr. Vallee, you are free to go home," he said. "You'll be more comfortable with your family." Dad perked up when Dr. Archer said he was officially released, but as he spoke to his physician his voice choked up, and I thought he might cry. "Thank you, Dr. Archer, I'm ready to go home."

"I can't thank you enough for your help, Doctor." I couldn't find the words to fully express my gratitude. "Thanks for the extra day in the hospital." I started to tear up, so I stopped talking.

Our compassionate doctor smiled at us and walked out the door. Our dry-eyed farewell was no less heartfelt than if we had shed copious tears.

Dr. Archer was our guiding star. He lit the way for a brief moment and then disappeared. In a candid conversation that was gentle, yet unambiguous, Dr. Archer told Dad that he was dying and that further treatment would make him feel worse. Dr. Archer's guidance set us on the path that gave us the freedom to let Dad live out his remaining days in peace.

"I need to get this room ready for the next patient," a young orderly said as he came into the room. "You have to leave." Dad put his legs over the edge of the bed and tried to stand up but fell back. He tried again and fell back again. The orderly waited; he wanted to strip the bed.

"Can we stay in here a little longer?" I asked, hoping he had noticed how weak Dad was.

"No, but I can help you move out into the hallway." We took what we could get. The orderly got on one side of Dad, and I got on the other. We settled him in a plastic chair in the hallway that was squeezed between a couple of carts stacked with trays of half-eaten food. Dad struggled to sit upright on the small chair.

"Everything is ready at home," I said, making small talk to pass the time. "The oxygen concentrator is huge, so I put it in the guest bathroom. The hospital bed looks fairly comfortable. I bought some new sheets from J. C. Penney that are extra long. Marlys suggested we get a foam pad for your wheelchair." He started to lean forward a little. I was afraid he would topple over. Nurses, aides, and orderlies were nearby to help if he slumped to the floor. Marlys came down the hall, walking quickly in our direction with a big smile on her face.

"Someone canceled! The Medi-Cab is available now. We can take Mr. Vallee home right away," she said. I felt a little less alone in the world now that I had Marlys to help me.

"This is Mr. Vallee," Marlys said to a couple of young men in dark blue uniforms. One pushed a wheelchair. I watched how it took both of them working together to get Dad in a standing position long enough to gently guide him into the wheelchair. Once he was settled, one man pushed the chair, the other carried Dad's bags, and I trotted along behind the procession, waving goodbye to Marlys.

Mom had done her job—the flag waved its welcome on the small back patio of the apartment.

"Watch your head, sir," the young man said as he tipped the chair back while the other man guided the lift down to the ground. Dad squinted against the sun. There would be no more clearing brush in the wash next to his house on Stony Ridge Road. No more motorized yard tools like his chipper shredder and chainsaw on a stick. No more joking about falling out of a tree, landing on his back, and waving his arms around like a turtle. Watching Dad in his wheelchair, leaving the natural world he loved so much, was agonizing.

The aides rolled Dad through the automatic doors and down the long hall to the apartment. As I led the little procession, I remembered that when Dad moved into Las Fuentes, he had told me he'd "go out the back door, in a box." Unspoken, but clearly implied was that the funeral home would take his body out the door. Dad had resisted moving to a retirement community because he knew it would be his last home. He was right.

"Welcome home!" Mom said as she opened the door and led the men to Dad's room.

"We are going to help you into bed now, sir." One of the aides made sure to describe what was going to happen before they made the transfer so there would be no mishaps. They expertly transferred Dad to the hospital bed and quickly departed. The bed dominated the room that was filled with antique furniture Dad had inherited from his parents. Earl and Anita's portraits were on the wall, stern faces watching us, making sure we didn't harm the heirlooms. A small Stiffel lamp I recognized from my grandparents' elegant home in Wisconsin stood near the bed.

"Smell that fresh air," I said, taking a deep breath.

A large window on one end of the room was open slightly, and the beige curtains fluttered in the breeze. Dad's bedroom was large. Even with the big hospital bed taking up so much space, it didn't feel crowded.

After the Medi-Cab attendants left, I felt abandoned. I knew it was irrational, but I wanted those two young men to stay and help me. Now it was just me and my parents, on our own.

"The place looks good," Dad said as he looked around the room. "I have to have this," he said as he held the wand from the suction machine, which was easily within his reach. I had put the huge oxygen concentrator in the guest bathroom adjacent to Dad's room because it made a little put-put sound that I knew would drive him nuts. The unit worked like a window air conditioning unit by taking in air, modifying it, and then delivering it in a new form. It was prescribed for Dad because he had low levels of oxygen in his blood. There was a hospital-style tray table on wheels that would provide a place for Dad to eat. A transfer bench was in the master bathroom so Dad could get in and out of the tub, and a commode (like a potty chair for grown-ups) for when he could no longer use the toilet.

The equipment was in place, Dad was in his bed, and Mom was by his side. I was relieved. When I had called Dr. Archer to ask him to help us talk to Dad, it was the beginning of his journey to a peaceful end of his life, at home with his family, in his own time. I started out not knowing what to do or how to do it, but every time I got stuck, a kind person reached out to help me. Dad was safe. No orderly could kick him out of his own room.

"We said goodbye to Dr. Archer when he signed Dad's release orders," I said to Mom.

"He's a good doctor," she said. None of us knew what to do next. We had never been in this situation before, and we'd need some time to feel comfortable with our new reality.

"I'll go order lunch," I said. They knew what was usually on the lunch menu.

"I want whatever soup they have," Dad said.

"I'd like cottage cheese and a banana," Mom said. She ate the same lunch every day.

"Dessert?" I asked. Las Fuentes had a dessert cart loaded with cakes, pies, brownies, cookies, and cream puffs. I was looking forward to a big piece of chocolate cake. They both wanted ice cream. Good idea—I'd have ice cream with my chocolate cake.

"You got it," I said. I went to the kitchen to place the lunch order but stopped in the foyer for a moment and looked back at my parents. After fifty-six years, their lives together would no longer be measured in years, but in days and hours. I could see the sadness descend on them as they sat together, waiting.

After I ordered lunch, I stayed in the kitchen. I thought about the days ahead that would end with my Dad going out the back door in a box.

CHAPTER 10

Promises to Keep

FTER LUNCH I GOT TO WORK on fixing the TV so the remote would work. Then Dad told me that the portable suction machine had less power than the one in the hospital, and he couldn't clear his throat. Mom pulled a muscle in her back when she put a blanket on Dad's bed.

Multiple scary scenarios swirled through my head as I contemplated how my parents would react to the arrangements I made for Dad's care. It would probably be Dad who got mad, but it could be Mom. She had made it clear that she would hire a minimum amount of professional help to take care of Dad. The worst would be both of them, asking me who the hell I thought I was, a humiliation that I could not bear. The home health aide was scheduled to come at 6:00 p.m. and stay all night. I was at the end of a diving board, bouncing up and down, waiting to jump.

The doorbell rang and I went to answer it. Valerie, tall and willowy, in a dress with fall colors of rust and gold, was here to tell my parents about the prescription service. My stomach was tied in knots as I took her to Dad's room. "Hello, I'm Valerie, from Assisted Living. Mr. Vallee, it's nice to see you settled at home." Dad smiled at her.

"Hello," Mom said, with a tentative smile.

"I'm here to tell you about the prescription service. It's starting today," Valerie said, smiling as she delivered the good news. "An aide will be by soon with your meds. Karina, our RN, will make sure your prescriptions are refilled. She'll work with your doctor's office if new prescriptions are written. You won't have to worry about a thing." Her tone was cheerful. My parents gave her a blank look.

"I signed you up for the prescription plan," I said, adopting my game show host persona again, describing the grand prize, hoping they'd be okay with it. I gave them a big smile and held my breath. Mom and Dad looked surprised, but not mad. Neither of my frugal parents asked, "how much?"

The awkward moment ended when the doorbell rang. I showed Valerie out and greeted the manager of Las Fuentes, Brian. He was a tall, athletic man who looked like a basketball coach, yet he had an affinity for working with the elderly.

"Mr. Vallee, it's good to have you back. The other residents and the staff have been asking about you," he said as he shook hands with Dad and smiled broadly at Mom.

Mom and Dad were clearly surprised that people had missed them. They had kept to themselves for decades; living at Las Fuentes had forced them to become part of a community. Eating in the dining room put them in proximity to their fellow residents, but they didn't join any of the social clubs. They didn't go on day trips in the van. Dad didn't shoot pool with the other men in the poolroom, and Mom didn't make a weekly trip to the on-site beauty shop or join a book club. Anne and I were the only people who visited them.

After Brian left, hospice nurse Marlys stopped by to see if Dad was settled.

"How are you doing, Mr. Vallee?" she asked.

"Better than in the hospital," Dad answered. "I'm glad to be out of there. I have everything I need right here." The stress and strain of his days in the hospital were lifting. He had been at home for only a few hours, but the change in his mood was palpable. He was free.

Marlys looked at me. "We're all set," I said with as much confidence as I could muster.

"Call me if you need anything," she said, satisfied that all was well. After Marlys left, we waited to see if the doorbell would ring again. It did. This time it was an aide from Assisted Living. She was an attractive young woman who wore her copper-colored hair in braids and had bright blue eyes and a cheerful smile. She carried Mom and Dad's first round of prescriptions. As I showed her to Dad's room, the knot came back in my stomach. But how could they resist this adorable young girl who looked like she just stepped out of a fairy tale?

"Hi, Mr. and Mrs. Vallee. I'm Jennie, here with your meds." She held a small tray with two paper cups on it, one for Mom and one for Dad. I got a couple of glasses, and Jennie filled them with water from the pitcher on the tray by Dad's bed.

"Bottoms up!" I said, as Mom and Dad swallowed their pills. I hoped my perky attitude would distract them from inquiring about the cost. They didn't ask any questions, even after Jennie left. Instead, we sat quietly, waiting for the doorbell to ring again, but the caravan of caring people had ended.

The TV in the bedroom sat on a small table. Dad's hospital bed was much higher than his regular bed, so the signal from the remote wouldn't reach the TV. I couldn't find anything in the apartment that was wide enough and flat enough to lift the set, so I walked across the parking lot to the maintenance garage. One of the guys gave me a piece of scrap wood, and as I headed back, I wondered how long Dad would want the TV. He couldn't see the screen; he could only listen.

My parents had five TV sets in the house on Stony Ridge Road and brought three to Las Fuentes. The TV was turned on as soon as they got up in the morning and was turned off just before they went to sleep. The morning started with local news from the station in Phoenix, and then they switched to CNN for the rest of the day. Wolfe Blitzer's *Situation Room* was a favorite, but the channel was changed in time for the television show *Jeopardy!* every evening at 7:00 p.m. When my parents went on cruises, Mom was known as "the brain" when she competed in a *Jeopardy!*-style game on board the ship.

As I headed back across the parking lot with my scrap of wood, Anne called. I put the wood down and fished my cell phone out of my pocket.

"Hi, Sis, how's it going?" It was good to hear her voice.

"I just got a piece of wood to put under Dad's TV so the remote will work. Lunch went pretty well. Mom and Dad know about the prescription service but didn't ask how much it would cost. So far, so good."

"I'm coming to Prescott tomorrow; we can talk more then," Anne said.

"See you soon, we have lots to talk about," I replied and then put the phone back in my pocket.

Anne and I would need to find some time to debrief. I'd show her the legal pad, and then we'd make plans for a future we couldn't imagine. The past week had been the most challenging of my life, and I was exhausted. I knew I could hand this off to Anne and not worry. We had become partners in our ten-year saga of providing care to our parents, and we trusted each other.

When I got back to the apartment, Dad wanted to talk to me about something more important than the TV. "I need to call the medical equipment store," he said. "I want a stronger suction machine. This one isn't working; it's not doing the job." One of my biggest concerns was Dad's choking, so I dialed the number for him.

"My name is Bob Vallee, and I have one of your suction machines. It isn't strong enough to clear my throat. Do you have a better one?" Dad's voice was strong, self-assured.

He was the father of my youth: in charge, solving a problem, handling it himself. He was still the king of his realm. He would say to his kids, only partly in jest, "I'm the king and you're nuthin'," which wasn't a self-esteem booster for young children, but we knew where we stood.

"They're going to send another unit tomorrow," Dad said after he hung up.

"That's good, Dad." After feeling powerless in the hospital, he was back at home and back in charge.

Dad became more relaxed and happy as the day went on. I was more relaxed, too, until he made a request. "I'd like to dine in the kitchen tonight, Kathy," he said, like I was a cruise director and he wanted to sit at the captain's table. I panicked.

The kitchen? I silently screamed. *He wants to eat in the kitchen! Sitting up? How the hell can he do that?*

I hadn't thought past getting Dad to the apartment and settled in bed. I was flummoxed at the thought of getting him from his hospital bed to the kitchen. I had watched nurses and the Medi-Cab attendants swiftly and skillfully move Dad where he needed to go, but they were trained professionals. He had no strength and flopped around like a rag doll when they moved him. I was just one middle-aged woman, and I knew Mom would be of no help.

If he fell when I tried to get him from the bed into the wheelchair, he could break his hip or hit his head. We would be back in the hospital, probably the ER.

"Kathy?" he looked at me like a kid who wanted to go to Disneyland for his birthday. Mom appeared in the doorway with Jennie, who was back with the next round of meds. I knew she was only supposed to bring the pills, but I asked her to help me with Dad.

"Mr. Vallee wants to have dinner in the kitchen," I said, "but I don't know how to help him into the wheelchair."

"Oh, that's simple," Jennie said cheerfully, "let me show you." Asking for help was getting easier and easier for me.

I got out of the way and watched her. Mom scurried out of the room. First, she put the rail down on the hospital bed.

Then she got the wheelchair lined up next to it. Very gently, she helped Dad sit up and twist around so his bony legs dangled from the edge of the bed. Jennie made sure the oxygen tubing didn't get kinked and the cannula (the small, two-pronged device, one for each nostril) didn't get pulled out. The tubing, looped around Dad's ears to hold the cannula in place, could easily be dislodged with the wrong move.

Jennie discreetly made sure Dad's robe kept as much of his torso and legs covered as possible. Once Dad was on the edge of the bed and his tubing was free, she put both her arms around his chest, bent her knees, and said authoritatively, "Stand up, Mr. Vallee!" He straightened his legs and, with her help, stood up and twisted around so that he could bend his knees again and sit down in the wheelchair.

Jennie let go of him, stood back, and said, "See? Easy." My eyes filled with tears as I thanked the sweet teenage girl who got me out of this jam. We had been home only a few hours, and everyone we met was kind and helpful. My fear of being on my own was gone. Mom, Dad, and I were surrounded with help. We only had to ask.

Dad, thrilled to be in his wheelchair, smiled and gave us the grimace and wink. Seeing his joy at eating dinner in the kitchen made the past few incredibly difficult days worth it. My Humpty Dumpty heart was being put back together again, one jagged piece at a time. I thanked Jennie again as she left and then pushed the wheelchair toward the kitchen.

When Jennie opened the door to leave, Jason, who worked in the dining room, maneuvered a meal cart through the door. When Jason saw Dad, he stopped. "Hi, Mr. Vallee, it's good to see you. We've missed seeing you and Mrs. Vallee in the dining room." The waiters were mainly kids from Prescott High School and were attentive and kind to the residents, who they must have assumed were a hundred years old.

"Jason," I said, "please help me figure out how to get Dad to the kitchen table." Mom sat at the far end of the table. I took the chair from the opposite end and sat in the middle. Jason maneuvered the wheelchair for Dad to reach the table. The bulk of the wheelchair jutted into the living room. We sat like tortoises in a burrow, wedged in tightly. Jason handed us our food and left. I felt relieved as I swiveled around to get drinks from the refrigerator as we began our first dinner at home.

Mom and I had chicken Parmesan, and Dad ate the food prepared by the kitchen staff to go down easily. We could identify the mashed potatoes and pureed peas and joked about what the other food was. It appeared to be some kind of meat.

"That looks worse than what they serve in a prison cafeteria," Dad said.

"How do you know what they serve in prison, Dad?" I joked. "This is Las Fuentes, for God's sake, not San Quentin."

"Pretty soon I'm going to have a martini," Dad proclaimed, with his spoon in mid-air. "We need to have happy hour."

"Sure, why not," I said. "You can have a martini whenever you want."

Now that Dad was in hospice, he was free. There were no more doctors telling him how large his martinis should be, or how often he should drink them. I reached into the small pantry and got out the gin, vermouth, and Dad's martini pitcher. Then I pivoted back to the refrigerator and poured a small amount of vermouth in the martini glass that was always in the freezer. I put gin and ice cubes in the martini pitcher and stirred. The olive jar was in the refrigerator door. I stabbed two of them with the red cocktail toothpick that looked like a sword. Then I carefully poured the gin in the martini glass, dropped the olives in, and handed it to my father.

"Welcome home!"

"I feel like we're at the Derby," Mom said.

"Yes!" Dad and I chirped in unison.

We loved the old-fashioned steak house in Arcadia, home of the Santa Anita racetrack. It was our kind of restaurant, with big booths upholstered in red leather, beamed ceilings, a huge fireplace and portraits of the famous jockeys who raced the ponies at the historic racetrack.

"Where is Vern when we need him?" I said.

Vern was the smooth-talking waiter whose quick wit kept us entertained when he took our order. We always finished off our meal with baked Alaska. Vern dramatically lit the brandy to set the dessert on fire, charring the meringue that topped the ice cream. Those memories of our sumptuous meals at the Derby floated above us in that cramped little kitchen like colorful balloons at a birthday party.

Right then and there, my parents and I were home. I was the mama bird, perched on the edge of a nest that was built, not with feathers, but with a hospital bed, an oxygen tank and suction machine, helpful teenage employees, and a hospice nurse. My two little chicks set their eyes on me. From the bottom of my soul I vowed to preserve this safe haven for as long as it took for Dad to die in peace.

The doorbell rang and I scooted out of my chair, squeezed past Dad's wheelchair, and opened the door. Dad's first caregiver, Ronnie, was at the door. She was an attractive middle-aged woman with bright red hair that formed a halo around her face.

"Honey, don't worry about your dad. I'm going to make sure everything is taken care of," she said. I was confident as I showed her our setup in Dad's bedroom. She asked to see the bathroom, so I took her to the master bathroom and told her there was a guest bathroom in the hallway with a big oxygen concentrator in the middle of it.

"Oh dear, I don't see any disposable gloves. I have to have them before I can help your dad get ready for bed," she said. My heart sank. Disposable gloves never crossed my mind. I had been so pleased when Dad enjoyed his martini and got his food down with no choking. Now there was a glitch.

It was 6:15 p.m., and I felt a slight panic rise in my throat, not knowing if the local drugstore stocked them. There were no twenty-four hour drugstores in town. Valerie would have some in her office in Assisted Living, but she was gone for the day.

"I'll find enough gloves to get you through the night," I said with fake confidence. "Let's go meet my parents." Once again Mom and Dad had blank looks on their faces when I told them Ronnie would be staying all night, and in the morning another aide would come to take her place.

I took her to the small nook just off the living room where she could put her coat, purse, thermos, and insulated lunch bag. It was small, but cozy, with a pullout sofa bed, a floor lamp, a small coffee table, and Dad's big rolltop desk. As I turned to go, Ronnie said, "Don't worry, sweetheart, I'll take good care of your folks."

I went back to my parents, who were still camped in the kitchen. "Ronnie needs to have disposable gloves before she can help you get back in bed," I said, looking only at Dad.

They both looked at me as if I had let a Martian in the apartment. They had hired a home health aide for four hours a day, and I had just told them Ronnie would stay overnight. They were either okay with it or too stunned to speak. I couldn't tell from the look on their faces, and didn't wait to find out.

"I'm going to run down to Assisted Living and see if they have some gloves," I said as I quickly walked away. I hoped they wouldn't tell Ronnie to leave before I got back. I sprinted down the hall to the Assisted Living wing. The night security guard, a high school kid, was at the desk. I was a little wild-eyed and must have scared him, because I had been running around all day solving problems, and now I didn't have any goddamn disposable gloves.

"Ronnie . . . my Dad's caregiver . . . doesn't have any disposable gloves. I have to get some right now . . . tonight, and I don't know what to do," I said, out of breath, my voice shaky.

"Hold on a minute, I'll check," he said. Without taking his eyes off me, he made a call, and a few moments later Jennie came around the corner.

"Jennie!" I screamed. I wanted to hug her but held back. "I need some disposable gloves for my dad's caregiver . . . please help me." I felt like an orphan begging for food.

"Mr. Vallee needs gloves? How many?" She had seen me a few times earlier that day and, wise beyond her years, understood that I was exhausted and desperate. I followed her back to the storage room, and she gave me a handful of medical-grade latex disposable gloves.

"Here," she said. "That should be enough until morning." I held back tears as I thanked her. I stared at the gloves as if they were nuggets of gold. "Thank you, Jennie, you saved me again."

When I got back, a miracle had happened. Ronnie had moved Dad to the living room in his wheelchair. Mom sat in the Medicare lift chair, and they were watching television, just as they had for the past fifty years. They nodded at me as I walked past them on the way to the nook, where Ronnie was reading a book. I handed her the disposable gloves. She was Annie Sullivan, my miracle worker.

Now that the TV was on, any conversation about the expense of home health aides could not take place. When the set was on, no one talked. I sat with Mom and Dad in the living room and relaxed. Soon I would be going back to the hotel. Dad was home and well cared for. Ronnie had made us comfortable. Mom was mellow, and I was more tired than I had been in my entire life. I knew for certain that the decision to bring Dad home was the right one. Then the phone rang.

Mom answered, looked up at me and mouthed the words, "It's Dick." She listened intently, beaming. My irritation returned in an instant, but I tried to hide it from my mother. Finally, she said goodbye and hung up.

"That was Dick," Mom said. "He was calling from the plane." I hoped my brother wasn't on his way to the airport in Phoenix. My vow to myself not to let him upset me was broken.

"He's with his girlfriend, and they are on the way to Cancun, Mexico, for a vacation," Mom said. My brother called my parents from an airplane, on the way to a vacation, less than twenty-four hours after learning his father was dying.

The thought of him walking through the door resurrected childhood memories of the times when he pushed me around, belittled me, and pulled me in to his schemes.

I began to pace back and forth, right in front of the TV. I needed to talk to Anne, so I walked to the foyer and called her. She had questions. "What else did Dick say? Is he coming to Prescott after his vacation?"

"I don't know, and I'm not sure I want to know. I can't think right now. I'm tired and just want to get some sleep," I said.

"Sis," she said very calmly, "Get out of there and go back to the hotel. Have a glass of wine and go to sleep. We'll sort this out tomorrow."

I went back to the living room. "Is Dick coming to visit?" I put it out there, like a hand grenade.

"He'll call when he gets back," Mom said. "He wants to see your father." Dad didn't say a word. His happy mood during dinner had vanished, and he sat facing the TV. I couldn't do anything about the strained relationship between Dad and Dick. I couldn't make Mom behave in the way I wanted her to, and I couldn't rewrite the history of my family.

I stopped by the nook and said goodbye to Ronnie. She assured me she'd get Dad settled for the night. There was no doubt Mom and Dad would be in good hands, so I said good night to them and left. As I drove back to the hotel that night, I concluded that I had the worst brother and the best sister in the world.

CHAPTER II

The Finances

O N FRIDAY MORNING I opened the blackout curtain in the hotel room, went out on the little patio, and let the sunshine wash over me. I sipped my tea, grateful that I didn't have to run off to meet a doctor, a hospice nurse, or a home health provider. My first task that morning was to find a box of disposable gloves. A week had passed since Anne called to tell me that Dad was not able to take his radiation treatments. It felt like a month.

I had been solely focused on accepting Dad's terminal illness, enrolling him in the hospice program, and making arrangements for his final days. I didn't expect that he would feel better, but his mood improved dramatically in the brief time he'd been home. The swelling in his throat decreased daily. We initially thought he'd pass on quickly, but now we had to reconsider. I wondered how long Mom and Dad would keep paying for home health aides. Anne and I had a lot to talk about.

I treated myself to eggs Florentine at Tall Pines coffee shop. It was quiet and had homestyle food. I lingered there for a while to enjoy a few minutes of relaxation in the quaint small town café.

When I got to Mom and Dad's apartment, the day-shift aide was sitting with Mom in the living room. They were talking like a couple of old friends. I suddenly realized the aides were going to be there as much for Mom as they were for Dad.

"Hi," I said. "I am Mr. Vallee's daughter, Kathleen. We are very happy to have you here."

"I'm Joan. Your dad is a pleasure to take care of," she said. "Sometimes the older men resent us, but your dad is a real gentleman." Mom was beaming. Joan added, with a wink, "I don't think he'll be too much trouble." Mom and I both smiled.

I hesitated before I went into Dad's room. There was still a slight chance Mom and Dad wouldn't want the home health aides, but from Mom's big smile, it looked like they would love them.

"Good morning, Dad," I said as I walked into his room. He had on fresh pajamas, was clean-shaven, and looked very content. Just twenty-four hours ago, he struggled to sit on a plastic chair in the hospital hallway. I kissed Dad on the top of his head and sat down on the gray Cabot wingback chair that had become the designated visitor's chair in Dad's room. It was very comfortable, so I sank into it and felt pretty content myself. It had been quite a week for all of us.

Before Dad could say anything, the phone rang. He picked up the receiver. It was my husband Paul, calling to see how he was doing.

"Where did you get such a good wife?" Dad asked my husband. "Kathy took care of everything, and I am now reclining in my bed at the home." Dad's voice was raspy, but he sounded like he had just brought home an Olympic gold medal. My gruff, authoritative Dad wasn't just praising me, he was *bragging* about me. I was shocked at first, then relieved, then flooded with emotions I had never felt before. He had never said anything like this before about me, in front of me, to anyone. Not only was he grateful to me for making all the arrangements, he was beaming with pride. For the first time in my life, my dad said he was proud of me.

Suddenly, role reversal felt pretty damn good. My dad, Bob Vallee, was giving me a standing ovation. Mom came into the room with a big smile on her face. The three of us had survived the roller coaster ride from radiation treatments for a hopeless cause to hope for a better way for Dad to live out his days. We knew there was a harrowing road ahead, but we had gotten this far, and all was well. The three of us enjoyed the moment.

I opened the window, and a fresh breeze rustled the curtains. After Dad hung up the phone, the moment of praise and glory passed, and he said he wanted to go to his desk to get his financial records. Dad's big rolltop desk was in the nook, on the other side of the apartment where the aides kept their belongings.

"Dad, I think it would be very hard to maneuver the wheelchair to the nook, and I doubt you could get the chair close to your desk. Tell me what you need, and I'll go get it," I said.

"The drawer on the right has hanging files. Bring the first six folders that are in that file. We'll start there."

As I went to get the files, I remembered the moment with Dr. Archer when Dad accepted his impending death and opted for hospice care. During that wrenching talk, I could not have imagined that Dad would be comfortable at home. If he had continued treatment, he'd be dead by now.

Hospice gave us time, but it wasn't just about Dad getting his financial affairs in order. Discussing money with the kids was a big Vallee taboo, and now Dad was casually breaking it. He trusted me, trusted my judgment. During Dad's time in hospice, he came to count on me. We overcame our lifelong, rock-hard inhibitions. On that sunny autumn morning, I felt like a grown woman who was getting to know her father as an adult, on equal terms.

We spent the morning going over Dad's files. He was satisfied that he had seen everything he needed to attend to.

"I need to talk to Laurel," he said. "My accountant."

Dad was notorious for his prejudice against women when it came to money, but it looked like the old dog had learned a new trick and found a competent female accountant. Since losing most of his sight, he couldn't see spread sheets. Mom still paid the bills, but Dad needed someone to look over his financial records and track his investments. He'd hired a new investment firm a year earlier, and his portfolio had shot up. The president of the company was his hero.

"Is it okay if I call Laurel's office?" I asked. Dad nodded. Laurel answered the phone and invited me to come over that afternoon. Dad was selecting the files he wanted me to take to her. What he said next surprised me.

"I need to go to the bathroom. Joan will help me."

"I'll go get her," I said and went to find Joan. I enjoyed my closer relationship with Dad but was relieved to have someone else take him to the toilet. I sat down with Mom in the living room.

"Mom, the aides from Helping Hands seem very nice," I said.

She nodded. "I'm glad they are here." She let out a big sigh.

"Hey, Mom," I leaned in close to her face and whispered, conspiratorially, "I'm relieved that neither of us has to take Dad to the toilet." Mom smiled and nodded. The doorbell rang and I went to answer it.

"Sis!" I said, "You're here!" I gave her the thumbs up sign, signaling that Mom and Dad were okay with the setup for Dad's medical care at home.

"That's great," she said with a smile as we went to the living room to see Mom.

Since Joan was there to help Dad with lunch, we three girls decided to go to the dining room to eat. Friday was Buffet Day at Las Fuentes, which included a big spread of soups, salads, meats, vegetables, and a huge assortment of desserts. Mom loaded her plate with deviled eggs while I grabbed a big piece of chocolate cake. Anne had rice pudding.

The three of us gabbed, just like the old days. Anne and I didn't mind when Mom told the story, for the one-hundredth time, about when Anne and I were pregnant at the same time and Mom had to stand outside restrooms every hour or two, waiting for us to go pee.

Mom was on a roll about the dual pregnancies, and Anne and I loved to reminisce about our first-born children, so we got on the memory train with Mom and listened to the story once again.

"Your father told you not to go into labor when we left for Chicago, Kathy. He wrote it on the blackboard in the kitchen," Mom said, with mock disappointment that I didn't comply.

I was living with my parents late in my pregnancy, because my husband was in Army basic training at Fort Polk, Louisiana. I delivered my daughter when my parents were in Chicago visiting Anne and her newborn son.

"I know, Mom," I said. "But I had the dog to keep me company when the contractions started."

My brother John, who had just become a licensed driver, drove me to the hospital. I got a big laugh when the nurse asked if he was my husband. He was sixteen! That part of the story always got a big chuckle.

After lunch, Anne and I went to Laurel's office with Dad's files. Her office was just off Whiskey Row, set back from the street, next to a small mountain stream. I loved the Old West feel of Prescott and the alpine atmosphere.

"Thanks for seeing us on such short notice," I said after we introduced ourselves. Laurel was an attractive woman in her early forties. She had started her own accounting firm after moving to Prescott. Dad seemed to think she had a big staff, but Laurel told us it was just herself and her assistant, Ann Marie.

"Dad trusts you," I said. "He has always kept his financial affairs private, but now he wants to include us."

"I'm so sorry," Laurel said. "I just started working with Mr. Vallee, and I didn't know he was so ill." On the conference room table was Dad's financial life, a well-kept secret, spread out bare.

"The most important thing for Dad is to make sure Mom has enough money after he's gone," Anne said.

"She will," Laurel said. "Your father was a wise investor. He made some very prudent choices, and your mother will be fine. Did you know she is trustee?"

"No!" Anne and I said in unison. We were surprised. "We'll talk to them about that," I said. "I don't know if Mom can manage; she's always been the bookkeeper, not the decision maker."

"You'll need to consult a lawyer to change it," Laurel explained. "I know a trust lawyer in town. He's one of the best in the state."

"We don't have much time," I said.

Laurel called Bernard Cross. When she explained the situation, he came over from his office across the street to meet us. Anne and I were grateful for Laurel's help. All we had to do was ask, and people came to our rescue. This new concept was sinking in.

After we explained our concerns about our mother being trustee, Bernard said he could draft an amendment to the trust. He asked who would replace Mom as trustee. My sister and I looked at each other for a moment, but we both knew it would be Anne. We thanked Bernard for seeing us on such short notice and took his card.

Anne and I were privy to Dad's finances, but amending the trust seemed way out of our newly constructed comfort zone. As we drove back to Las Fuentes, we agreed that this was a two-daughter task and were glad we were together to accomplish it. Neither of us thought Mom would want to be trustee. She didn't want to make big decisions; she just wanted to be taken care of.

That evening the four of us sat together in Dad's room after dinner. The Stiffel floor lamp cast its light gently in the room and softened the atmosphere. I kept looking at the portraits of Earl and Anita on the wall. My grandparents were more alive and real to me as I watched my dad die than they had been when I was a child. I looked at the stern picture of Grandpa and remembered how afraid I was of him. My unsmiling grandmother was a handsome woman, with her pearl necklace and earrings. She had scared me too.

Our conversation was casual and light, with some corny jokes and memories of our childhood. We didn't discuss anything of an emotional nature, but we felt connected in our own way. Our nonverbal communication was more fluent than the words we spoke. I soaked up the warm, loving feelings; we felt safe with one another.

Mom gratefully relinquished trustee status with many thanks to Anne for taking on the job. Anne said she'd call Bernard and ask him to draft whatever needed to be done. I didn't expect Mom to object to Anne being trustee, but I was relieved when she so quickly agreed.

Dad's stocks had increased substantially in the last quarter. He mentioned several times that he was glad he had hired an investment firm in Phoenix. I didn't know much about the firm, or the big guru, but was glad Dad had peace of mind.

"Hey, Dad," I said, "do you want to send him a letter? I'll write it for you on your computer." He liked that idea.

I got a notepad from his desk, sat on the chair by his bed, and adjusted the floor lamp so I could see. He spoke in a falsetto voice, almost childlike, and his words were sports-fan caliber as he thanked the investment manager who grew his money.

"My statements for the third quarter have grown substantially, and I am pleased at their speedy progress upward. Your company has exceeded my expectations, and I am grateful and proud to be part of your organization. If your exemplary performance continues, as I'm sure it will, I will be a very happy man."

The rest of the letter continued with Dad's praise of the company and his appreciation of the client account coordinator and the investment counselor.

I wrote the letter on his computer and then went back to read it for Dad's final approval. He signed the letter, and I promised to drop it in the mail. It was our last father/daughter project.

Anne and I said good night and went back to the hotel. We sat together in the lobby with a bottle of wine between us.

"You've got your work cut out for you, Sis," I said. "Lots going on."

"I sure do. As soon as Bernard drafts the trust document, I'll set an appointment for him to come to Las Fuentes so Mom and Dad can sign it. I'm going to ask Laurel to be there, too, so we can make sure all the finances are in order. It will be my top priority."

"Check with Patti to see when the Helping Hands bill is due and make sure Mom is ready with a check." I said. "The September rent is also due and includes the cost of the prescription service. Mom needs to pay that too. I don't know how much cash they have on hand, or the balance in the checking account. I know they have more than one account, maybe as many as five."

"Got it," said Anne. "You are right, they have five checking accounts."

"There is a big foam pad in the storage room that you can cut to fit Dad's wheelchair. We should have some coupons on hand for guests in the dining room, just in case Dick and Jean show up. The oxygen concentrator needs a new key, but the company will bring one. Dad can have a martini whenever he wants one; ice cream too. Be sure to keep the air conditioner on in Dad's room at night. I have both our phone numbers by the phone and told the aides to call us if Mom or Dad try to discontinue the service. Mom's bedspread needs to be picked up at the cleaners. At some point we'll have to start thinking about the funeral." There was more, but I stopped. I had a list of more tasks on the legal pad, but it could wait till tomorrow.

"I'll get started first thing in the morning," Anne said as she took another sip of wine.

I didn't envy her.

CHAPTER 12

The Miracle of Pastor Dan

ANNE COMPLETED ALL THE financial arrangements during the week she was in Prescott. She met with Bernard, Laurel, Mom, and Dad at the apartment and was legally named as trustee. Anne became a signer on the main checking account and helped Mom close the other four. She left on Friday, exactly two weeks after Dad's decision to leave the hospital and return home with hospice care.

After Anne and I had each spent a week in Prescott, Mom and Dad were well cared for and the finances were set. It was my turn to go see them. After I learned that Dick was planning a visit, I drove over after he'd gone and planned to stay a few days.

Dick had come on Saturday and stayed for two hours. Just over six feet tall, Dick was slender for a fifty-five-year-old and was classically handsome, with well-defined features and piercing blue eyes. He knocked his dignified looks down a peg when he started dying his hair, which made him look like a character in the *Addams Family* TV show. Still, he must have been a dashing figure when he and Mom lunched together in the dining room. Neither Anne nor I knew what they discussed, but if there had been a big fight, we thought Mom would have told us. No news was good news.

Mom and Dad got attached to the Helping Hands caregivers. They kept Mom company and took care of Dad. Dad gave them nicknames, based on what they did for him: Muffin Lady brought him breakfast, Soup Lady brought him lunch, and Pee Lady took him to the toilet. The aides from Assisted Living delivered their meds four times a day. The constant support from Helping Hands and the Las Fuentes staff enabled my parents to establish a smooth rhythm in their lives.

I parked in the back of the building and walked slowly down the hall to my parents' door. I stood there but didn't ring the bell. I had kept in touch by phone, but now I would be face-to-face with Dad, and I didn't want to see him weaker and sicker. I was afraid to see him closer to death.

During my last visit, a little over two weeks ago, Mom, Dad, and I had made a huge decision, and it turned out to be the right thing to do. Then there was a myriad of tasks to complete. I was at my best with a to-do list in hand and had done everything to make sure my parents were cared for. Now we were just waiting.

I dreaded seeing Dad and wondered if this would be the last time I'd see him alive. I was afraid he'd die while I was there; I didn't want to see his dead body. I was more scared than sad, and felt childish. I took some deep breaths to calm myself down and finally rang the doorbell. Mom answered. I followed her to the living room and felt relieved to see Dad's bedroom door was closed.

Mom looked pretty good, though there were some food stains on her blouse, and her hair needed to be washed. She had been in the apartment for several days with no break. I planned to take her out that weekend to do some shopping and have lunch at Tall Pines coffee shop. Mom didn't have a standing appointment at Las Fuentes Beauty Salon, so I'd try to make one for her.

"How are you doing, Mom?" I asked. She pushed her dirty hair back from her forehead, let out a big sigh, looked down at the carpet, and said, "fine."

"How did it go with Dick?" I asked.

"Your father was glad to see him. They talked." Her voice was dull and full of fatigue. There was no mention of how the visit went with Dick. I could tell she didn't want to discuss it any further, so I dropped it.

"How is Dad?"

"He's talking to the pastor," Mom said.

"Pastor?" I didn't think I heard her right. "You mean a preacher . . . a man of God?"

"It's part of the hospice service," she said. "They send a preacher automatically, and when he showed up your father said he would talk to him. They have been in there for more than an hour."

"Dad? Bob Vallee, who only stepped inside a church when one of his kids got married? That Dad?" I played it up.

"Yes, that Dad," Mom smiled. As much as I annoyed her, I could also make her laugh. It was good to see her smile.

"Wow, Dad talking to a preacher for more than an hour," I said. "I wonder what they are talking about. Dad doesn't talk about God unless he hits his finger with a hammer."

She laughed again. We were a religiously unaffiliated family, and Mom and I enjoyed a little joke about Dad and the preacher on a morning when there really wasn't much to laugh about. Then I had an idea.

"Hey, Mom, let's ask the preacher to read John's letter to Dad," I said. We still hadn't thought of who would read the letter, but now we had a perfect person, and we could get that job done. A preacher couldn't say no to a request like that; it's what preachers did.

"Okay," she agreed. "Good idea."

"I'll ask him today," I volunteered.

"Why don't you go in there?" she said. "I don't think they'd mind."

I got up and headed to Dad's room. I wanted to meet the pastor who managed to engage Dad in conversation for more than an hour. It would be easier to see Dad with another person in the room, especially a preacher, but I couldn't bring myself to go in. I heard the oxygen concentrator in the guest bathroom going put-put-put. I dug down, found some courage, and knocked on the door.

"Come in." My father's raspy voice gave me permission to enter.

Dad's complexion was grayer and his skin sagged, but the blue lines from the radiation were almost gone. The window was open, and a gentle breeze filled the room with fresh air.

He was clean-shaven, and his hair was combed back in his usual style.

The pastor looked old enough to be retired. The Hospice Family Care job was on an as-needed basis, so he may have been semi-retired. His clothes were cowboy casual, and he wore a Western-style shirt with khaki pants and desert boots. Dad wouldn't have related to a preacher dressed in black.

"Hi, Dad," I said. Pastor Dan stood and extended his hand to me.

"I'm Pastor Dan from Hospice Family Care." He shook my hand and offered me the designated visitor's chair, but I opted to sit on the other side of Dad's bed. I felt as if I were intruding and realized that Dad didn't have anyone to talk to privately, man-to-man, since his fateful discussion with Dr. Archer.

Anne and I had each other, but Dad must have felt he couldn't discuss his thoughts and fears with Mom or the aides. It was obvious he had found someone to talk to in Pastor Dan. Maybe he was talking about the estrangement with Dick and Jean. I decided to stay long enough to make small talk and then get out of there.

"We were just talking about how many more people are being cremated these days," Dad said. Pastor Dan cited some statistics about the increase in cremation and said it was much cheaper than burial. The pastor was talking in my Dad's language, practical and economical. Dad was discussing the disposal of his dead body with the pastor. I anticipated small talk, but this wasn't small talk; this was monumental, slightly creepy talk. The pastor and Dad were talking about cremation as if they were discussing how many more people are eating whole grains or using bouncy houses at birthday parties.

Once I collected my wits about the unexpected conversation going on in Dad's room, I excused myself and went back to the living room.

Mom and I enjoyed our ladies' day out. We ate lunch at Tall Pines, and Mom agreed that their food was good. There were no deviled eggs on the menu, so Mom broke out of her usual routine and ordered a hamburger and fries. We went to the bookstore, and she stocked up on paperbacks.

"Look! I found two Philippa Gregory books," Mom said, clutching them to her chest. Reading historical novels had always been her escape.

Our last stop was the grocery store. "I'll be right back, I only need a few things," Mom said. She wanted to go by herself. We needed a break from one another, so I sat at the front of the store and waited. She leaned heavily on the cart, pushing it slowly up and down the aisles, and came back with a package of toilet paper, a jumbo pack of paper towels, orange juice, and three bags of Hershey's Miniatures. She wrote a check at the checkout stand while the cheerful clerk and bagger chitchatted with her. For that brief moment Mom was back in her element, doing a job she had done for the past fifty-six years.

When we got back to the apartment, Pastor Dan was gone, but his business card was on the hutch in the foyer. I called and left a message for him to call me back. I wanted to ask him as soon as possible to read John's letter to Dad.

I needed to do something about Dad's car. I called the car dealer in Phoenix, and he remembered Dad right away. I was getting to know my Dad through the people he knew, and they all had a high regard for him. The car dealer said he'd terminate the lease and offered to send someone to retrieve the car. More help from people we didn't know. Not only was I getting used to asking for help, I started to count on it.

Cars were core to Dad's identity and independence. Giving up his last Lincoln Town Car was painful. Had he not been in hospice, he would have held out hope that he could drive again, a false hope that he would have held on to until he died.

The next day, Mom and I filled out the pre-need form for the funeral home and began to discuss the service. Dad wanted to be cremated, so I checked that box on the form. In keeping with his wish to go out in a box, I also put a checkmark next to the cheapest container for his remains, which cost eighty dollars. It was basically a cardboard box.

We knew Pastor Dan would lead the service, but I wanted to pick some readings. Anne had a friend who wanted to say a prayer, and that was okay with Mom. Although she never looked back after she left the Catholic Church, Mom didn't mind if Anne and I added some mildly religious content to Dad's service. I had a book of psalms and poems and chose some I thought Mom would like. We sat together that evening in the kitchen and I read a few lines, then looked at Mom, and she would shake her head "yes" or "no." There was a poem by Yehuda Halevi that we both liked.

'Tis a Fearful Thing

'Tis a fearful thing
to love what death can
touch.

A fearful thing
to love, to hope, to
dream, to be—

to be,
And oh, to lose.

A thing for fools, this.

And a holy thing.

a holy thing
to love.

For your life has lived in
me,
your laugh once lifted
me
your word was gift to
me.

To remember this brings
painful joy.

'Tis a human thing, love,
a holy thing, to love
what death has touched.

It was a taboo-breaking moment, and one of the most tender I ever had with my mother. Reading the selections for the funeral made both of us vulnerable. The words were beautiful, ancient, and meant to comfort, but Dad was in bed in the other room, still alive, and we were already giving words to our grief. Both of us were submerged in pain.

Mom went to her bedroom to look for something in her closet, a huge walk-in with wire shelves. The wire shelves looked flimsy and reminded us that Las Fuentes was a facility that was designed for a regular turnover in residents. The closets in my parents' home on Rocky Ridge Road had sturdy wood shelving, built to last.

When Mom didn't come back, I went to her bedroom to look for her. She was standing in her closet with her back to me.

"Mom," I said softly, "What are you looking for?"

"This doesn't look good," Mom said as she turned to look at me. I had a feeling she forgot what she went there to find. We stood and looked at each other, and then she started to cry; really cry, she was sobbing. I went over and hugged her, and she held on to me like a little kid on the first day of kindergarten. Then I did something that surprised me. I cried too. Mom and I stood in the closet and cried together, just like we did the night I read John's letter. But these were tears of grief, tears of the gut-wrenching fear of death. We were walking through the valley of the shadow of death. We held on to each other.

I couldn't think of anything to say to comfort my mother, or myself. Mom went into the bathroom and closed the door. I went back to the living room and put the psalms book away. We both needed some time alone, to recover from such an intense moment. I didn't want to leave her yet, so I looked in the pantry to see if there were any good bottles of wine. There was a half-empty bottle of red wine, just enough to fill a wine glass for both of us. I found a rerun of *The Golden Girls* that we watched together without much laughter. After the show was over, I went back to the hotel.

The next day Laurel's assistant, Ann Marie, came to the apartment to go over the bills with Mom. Ann Marie was very patient with her, and they decided together which bills Mom would pay and which ones Ann Marie would handle. They agreed that Mom would put the bills in a shoebox. Ann Marie would come once a week and they would look at them together. Mom was getting used to having help too.

I arrived at the apartment Monday morning. Mom and I sat together for a while in the living room. I looked at her tired face and felt guilty for leaving. I knew Dick and Jean planned a visit later in the week. I didn't want to go into Dad's bedroom. I knew it would be the last time I would see him alive. I had a long drive ahead of me, and I couldn't delay much longer. Finally, I got up and walked into Dad's room.

Caroline, Dad's aide for the day shift, had given him breakfast. I told her I'd sit with him a while. She said he had asked for ice cream. Marlys told us one of the signs of impending death was lack of appetite, but Dad seemed to be hungry all the time. Now that his throat was back to normal, he wanted lots of ice cream. I went to the kitchen and got one of the ice cream cups from the freezer and a spoon.

"Dad," I put my hand on his shoulder, but he didn't respond. "I'm going to give you some ice cream." He nodded but didn't open his eyes. I started spooning little bites of vanilla ice cream into his mouth. As soon as he swallowed, he opened his mouth for more, like a baby bird.

I looked at his hands, folded over his chest and felt sad when I saw the white band of skin on his left hand where his Vallee family ring used to be. It had his three initials—RLV—Robert Louis Vallee.

I put the empty ice cream container in the waste basket and sat down in the wingback chair by my father's bed. No words came to me, and I didn't know if he could hear me if I spoke. I tried to meditate, to communicate without words, but nothing came. The past three weeks were the most intensely lived, and the most emotionally satisfying and enriching time I had ever known with my parents. I would miss that as much as I'd miss my dad.

My job was done. Neither Dad nor I had quit in the middle of it. We had we forged ahead in spite of fear and uncertainty, and now Dad was ready. I leaned over, kissed his cheek, and said, "I love you, Dad."

He nodded his head but didn't seem to be able to open his eyes. I was glad, because I didn't want to see their wild rotation. I held his hand for a moment and then left the room. The grief my mother and I shared the previous night prepared me for this moment. Grief had grabbed Mom and me by the throat, but we continued on. It was time for me to go. I walked out of Dad's room.

I said goodbye to Mom and headed home. I loved the drive through Prescott National Forest. As I drove, I remembered all the times my family had traveled through Skull Valley on our way to visit Mom and Dad. The next time I would come this way, it would be for Dad's funeral. It looked like rain; the sky was gloomy with storm clouds coming over the mountains. Raindrops began to splatter on my windshield as I headed for the interstate.

My sister and I did not return to see our parents after I left that day. Dick and Jean were scheduled to visit early the next week. I wondered if they might be too late. As alienated as I was from Jean, I still hoped she'd get a chance to see Dad before he died. Forty-eight hours after Jean's visit, Dad passed away in his sleep early in the morning of September 26, 2000.

CHAPTER 13

Safe Passage

M Y CELL PHONE BUZZED me awake at 5:00 a.m. on the morning of September 26. I fumbled for the phone, trying to wake up enough to answer it. My husband woke up too. We both knew it was Anne with the news of Dad's passing.

"Hello," I said.

"Sis, Dad is gone. His overnight aide Ronnie called at 3:00 a.m. Ronnie stayed with Mom till the mortuary took Dad away and then she left, so Mom is alone. I'm leaving for Prescott soon."

"Mom is alone?" I asked, even though Anne had just told me she was. I had trouble comprehending what my sister was saying. If Mom is alone, where is Dad? I felt like a little kid who lost her parents in a department store.

"I'll get there as soon as I can," I said. I fell back on my pillows and tried not to think, but my mind was swirling. Where was Dad now? I knew he was physically at the mortuary, but where was his spirit?

"See you in Prescott," Anne answered.

"I'm sorry, honey," Paul said. "It's hard to believe your dad is gone. I know you want to leave as soon as possible."

"Yes. I need to leave a message at work. The car is low on gas. I'll need to pack something to wear for the funeral." I was talking about what I was going to do, but I couldn't get out of bed. I wanted to go back to sleep and not go through this.

"I'll take your car to the gas station," Paul said.

"Thanks." I was grateful for his kindness. It gave me courage to start the day. An hour later I got on Interstate 10 and called Anne. It was an overcast day. The gloomy weather matched my mood.

"I talked to Mom, and she told me what happened." Anne gave me the details. "Ronnie confirmed that Dad was dead when she checked on him at 2:00 a.m. She told Mom the end was near the night before and asked if she wanted to stay in Dad's room, but Mom didn't want to."

"That probably has to do with losing her mother at a young age and seeing her in the casket. Mom always said that she saw a lot of death when she was young and didn't want to see more," I said. I pictured my mother alone in her apartment.

"It's good that Ronnie made the calls to the mortuary and to me. It would have been too hard for Mom. Ronnie didn't leave until she knew I was on the road."

"Ronnie is a very kind person. She was the first aide to take care of Dad, and she was also the last," I said, feeling lost, forlorn and empty.

"The Helping Hands aides were a band of angels," Anne said, "and now they are gone. I'll be in Prescott in about thirty minutes." I had four more hours on the road.

The long drive gave me time to absorb the reality of Dad's death and to wonder how we would get through the next few days. The completed pre-need form for Ruffner-Wakelin Funeral Home was on the hutch in Mom and Dad's apartment. I planned to use Dad's computer to write an outline for the memorial service. Working on my to-do list was comforting.

I got off the interstate and kept the car at eighty miles-per-hour on the old two-lane highway through Skull Valley. The sun came out, and the sky was vibrantly blue. It was irrational, but I craned my neck and looked up through the windshield to see if Dad was there, in a clear blue heaven. When I reached the part of the highway that went through the mountains, my cell phone rang. It was Anne.

"Dick's here." Her voice was flat and urgent.

"What? Why?" I asked, as if she would know the answer. The jumbo-size bag of Cracker Jack in my lap tipped over, and the candy-coated kernels started to tumble to the floor. Damn.

"He showed up at the front door, just after I arrived." She was whispering. "After I called you, I called John and asked him to tell Dick and Jean about Dad. Dick must have left his home in Las Vegas immediately and driven to Prescott."

"What does he want?" I asked. I was frustrated about the Cracker Jacks and angry at my brother.

"I don't know," she said. "He and Mom have been sitting in the living room. She seems happy to see him. They're talking about Dad."

"When is he leaving?" I asked.

"I don't know, and I don't want to ask." Anne was on edge.

"I'll be there in about two hours," I told her, "maybe he'll be gone by then."

"Hope so," she said, "They want to go down to the dining room for lunch. I made a 4:00 p.m. appointment at Ruffner-Wakelin to make arrangements for the funeral and cremation."

What motivation did Dick have to show up the day our dad died, after all the years of bitter estrangement? Could they have reconciled during their two brief visits? Did they ignore the decades of silence and talk about Dick's business, while Dad was on his deathbed? I'd never know.

Two hours after Anne's call I arrived in Prescott, parked in the back, climbed over the railing of the small porch, opened the door, and walked into the apartment. Mom and Dick sat together in silence. Anne was in the manager's office. Mom stood up when I came in, and we embraced. She was shaking.

"We'll get through this, Mom," I said. She didn't speak, just nodded. I could tell she was close to shedding forbidden tears. The tears we had shed together in the weeks before Dad died were ours alone. Mom would not cry in front of Dick.

During my drive, I had been thinking about Dad in spiritual terms, but now I was confronted with the physical reality of my shocked and grieving mother. I saw, and sensed, her overwhelming grief.

Dick and I acknowledged one another; appraising each other silently, like a couple of predatory animals. We hadn't seen each other for at least fifteen years, and we both looked older but perhaps not wiser, at least in regard to our opinion of one another. Anne came back, and I excused myself to go freshen up before we went to the funeral home.

Ruffner-Wakelin was a family business, housed in a big Victorian house with lots of homey touches. From the front porch, we could see the stately courthouse in the middle of Prescott's town square, bordered by Whiskey Row, in the heart of Prescott's tourist district.

Dick drove by himself. Anne, Mom, and I drove over in Anne's car. Anne and I were vocal in our speculation about why our brother would appear on Mom's doorstep and insert himself into this most intimate process.

"What was that line from Tennessee Williams about funerals and death?" I asked, from the back seat.

"Funerals are pretty compared to death," Anne said in a perfect Southern accent. *A Streetcar Named Desire*.

"That's it, Dick has shown up for the pretty part," I said.

"He's here," Mom said. "Let's just make the best of it." She kept her statement neutral, knowing how tense Anne and I were, and she didn't want to set us off on a tangent against Dick. We took the hint and changed the subject.

Ruffner-Wakelin Funeral Home was behind schedule, so we were asked to wait for a few minutes. Alice, the funeral assistant, would be here soon. Dick arrived shortly after we did, and the four of us were very uncomfortable as we sat on the side porch. I held the pre-need form in my hand, ready to go, wanting to get it over with.

It had always been the three of us: Mom, Anne, and me, who had slogged through the illnesses and the endless rounds of medical treatments. We didn't always agree, and we weren't always kind to one another, but we stuck together. Now we had Dick with us, slumped on the couch next to his newly widowed mother. He just didn't belong.

Alice came at last and took us out to the converted garage that was now a showroom, with urns and coffins and headstones. I handed her the pre-need form. When Alice suggested a coffin, I pointed to the pre-need form and said Dad wanted a cardboard box. Pointing to a form and insisting on a cardboard box to put my Dad's body in was hard. I thought Alice would consider me to be a cheap, miserly daughter who didn't want to put her dad's body in a decent coffin; but I knew Dad, and what he wanted was a cardboard box.

Alice told us the crematorium was out at the edge of town and they would take Dad there tomorrow. We could pick his ashes up on the day of the funeral. I began to absorb the reality of Dad's death in little jabs of pain that struck suddenly and without warning. Tears began to well up, but there was no way I would cry now, in front of everyone. We Vallees got through it, dry-eyed and businesslike. We kept our feelings stuffed down, out of sight.

Then Alice took a deep breath, clasped her hands together and said, "Tell me about Bob Vallee." She looked at the four of us, and we stared back, our faces blank.

"He was a good father," I said.

"Yes," Anne said. "He was a good husband too."

Dick had a glassy-eyed stare. His expression was frozen; he didn't agree or disagree when Anne and I went on about what a good dad and grandfather Bob Vallee was. He didn't say anything.

At the end of the meeting, Alice presented each one of us with a tiny butterfly pin. She told us how our father had flown away, but would soon become a chrysalis, assume another shape in another dimension—or something like that. She was very kind. She couldn't know, as she pinned the butterfly on Dick's lapel, of the acrimony that had festered and grown between father and son over the years.

After we left Ruffner-Wakelin, we went to the Western Wrangler for dinner. It was a burger joint, and Anne, Mom, and I ordered burgers and fries. Dick ordered the Bacon-Bacon Cheeseburger and the Saddlebag Burger, a double order of fries, and a chocolate milkshake. It was his habit to eat two entrées because, he claimed, he worked so hard he burned enough calories for two people.

Everyone was tense. I wanted to get some casual conversation going, for Mom's sake, but couldn't think of anything to say. Then I thought of a question.

"When are you leaving Dick?" I asked. I wanted to know if he planned to stick around for the funeral. He was busy gobbling down his food. He spoke before he finished chewing, a habit he had continued since childhood.

"I gotta get back to work," he growled. There was a big glob of barbeque sauce on his chin and something black between his front teeth. "I'm leaving after we eat."

I knew Mom also wondered when Dick would leave, but I could see that she disapproved of my question, and I felt bad for upsetting her. Still, the three us wanted to know if Dick would be staying on; he upset our rhythm.

We said goodbye to Dick in the parking lot. As he drove away I wondered if I would ever see him again. As much as I disapproved of the way Dick treated Dad, I hoped my brother and father got some closure during their two short visits.

We drove back to Las Fuentes, and Anne and I stayed with Mom for a while in the apartment. I needed to call the medical equipment store first thing tomorrow and ask them to pick up the bed and oxygen concentrator. For now, Anne and I wanted to make sure Mom was okay by herself. Dad was gone, and the aides who had kept her company for the past twenty-nine days were gone too.

"I'm okay, girls," Mom said. "Really. I'm okay."

My sister and I drove to the hotel, not quite convinced Mom would be okay, but we had no choice but to take her word for it.

CHAPTER 14

Memorial and Farewell

D AD'S MEMORIAL SERVICE took place in the parlor of the Ruffner-Wakelin Funeral Home at 10:00 a.m. on September 29, 2000. The parlor had many frilly touches: mirrors with round frames, red velvet chairs, prints of smiling cowboys, and lace doilies everywhere. The atmosphere in the room was informal and didn't feel like a church. Dad would like that.

"Where is the table for Dad's mementos?" Anne asked. We had brought some things we thought he would have liked for the service. She had Dad's straw gardening hat, a little brass dog he loved, and one of his oldest woodworking tools, to place on the small round table he made in shop class when he was in high school in 1938.

"Ben is getting it from the car," I replied. "He's bringing in the pictures too." My son went to the car to get the things we needed for the service. My daughter Autumn was with Mom at Las Fuentes and would bring her to Ruffner-Wakelin before the service.

The pictures were of Mom and Dad, one on their fiftieth wedding anniversary, another one from a cruise to Alaska, with Mom in a fancy dress and Dad in a tuxedo, both looking very pleased with themselves. Anne brought a photo of Dad when he was a baby, sitting outside on a blanket, squinting into the sun. I remembered Dad squinting at the bright sun the day he came home from the hospital. My constant companion, grief, poked hard at me again.

There were several bouquets of flowers from family, friends, and coworkers. I gave a copy of the outline of the service to everyone who was scheduled to speak. Anne asked her friend Doug to read the poem Mom and I selected, "'Tis a Fearful Thing," by Yehuda Halevi. I asked Paul to read the Twenty Third Psalm. Pastor Dan would allow some time for people to talk about their memories of Dad toward the end of the service. Funeral Director Jeff had cued up a CD of Mario Lanza singing "Danny Boy." Jeff gave us programs that Alice, our funeral assistant, had prepared for the service. Everything was ready.

Once we were all set, Jeff told us he would videotape the service and give us a copy, free of charge. It seemed a little strange at the time to videotape a funeral, but it became a precious document of Dad's life.

Pastor Dan arrived, and I handed him the outline for the service. Mom came in on Autumn's arm, looking very tired and slightly disoriented. There was a small alcove to one side of the room, and Mom, Anne, and our husbands sat there. Anne's children, Paul and Thea, sat with their cousins,

Ben and Autumn, in the middle of the room. Las Fuentes manager Brian was there, as well as Laurel the accountant, some of Dad's home health aides, and several residents of Las Fuentes.

The service would begin in a few minutes. Anne and I sat on either side of Mom. Each of our children would speak during the service about their memories of Grandpa Bob. Absent from this gathering were Mom's other children, Dick, Jean, and John. She had done her best to raise all five of us, but her devotion was not returned on this day by three of her five children.

Pastor Dan took his place at the front of the room. He had known my dad for a brief time, but he ministered to him in the truest sense of the word. A single chime began to ring. It rang, over and over, a lonely note that heralded the beginning of the service. Mom began to cry. Anne leaned over and touched her arm. She was so deep in grief that she cried openly in public.

"We are here today to celebrate the life of Bob Vallee." Pastor Dan said. I was nervous because I would be the first to speak. Pastor Dan nodded to me as I approached the podium. I looked into his kind eyes and was grateful that we had a steady guide to help us through this mingling of celebration, grief, gratitude, and loss.

I took a deep breath, and started to read my eulogy. "I stood with Mom and Dr. Archer in the hospital at the moment Dad accepted his fate. He would gladly have suffered more pain if he thought for one minute he could stay around a little longer to take care of Mom. We gave him permission to go, and he accepted it with courage, in his inimitable style. Always a classy guy, he remained so till the end."

I put memories of Dad as a grandfather in my eulogy. "Immediately after Autumn was born, I lived with Mom and Dad for two months. Every evening I wheeled her little basket into the living room where she slept while we watched television. When she got older, she would sit with Dad in his easy chair and watch *The Lawrence Welk Show* on Saturday night. Twenty-two years later, Mom, Dad, and I met in Albuquerque to attend Autumn's art show at the Richard Levy Gallery. Although the art on display was something he really couldn't relate to, he was proud of his granddaughter."

"Ben," I began, "was a dynamo as a toddler and learned to walk at nine months. When he was about a year old, we were at Mom and Dad's house, and Ben ran so fast he became airborne. Eventually he crashed, and started to cry. Twenty-three years later, my grown son walked with his grandpa, ever so carefully, into the emergency room at Methodist Hospital on Thanksgiving night."

I paused for a moment; that memory was so painful I stopped speaking. I took a deep breath and continued. "Dad was so sick from the chemotherapy that we had to admit him. It was Ben who went home, got the turkey and trimmings, and brought it all back to the hospital. We devoured our dinner, gathered by Dad's bedside. Ben learned first-hand from his grandpa how men take care of things."

Then it came time to thank my sister. "When push came to shove," I said, " it was my older sister Anne who became my partner when Mom and Dad needed care. I cannot imagine getting through the last seven years without her and will always be grateful for her support, love, and understanding."

I was holding up pretty well, not stopping to cry, so I wrapped up. "Although the past few years, and especially the last few months, have been stressful, I wouldn't have traded them for the world. I would not have missed the opportunity to help Dad get dressed the day he left the hospital for the last time or to give him a 'bear hug' in order to lift him from his wheelchair. I wouldn't have traded one day, one conversation, one hysterical moment." I finished my eulogy and went back to my seat.

Pastor Dan returned to the podium, visibly emotional, as he began to read the letter John wrote to Dad. "This is the second time I've read this letter from son John. The first time was to his mother and father. There were tears then, and I hope I can get through this now." Pastor Dan took a deep breath to compose himself.

I wasn't there when the pastor read John's letter to Mom and Dad at Las Fuentes, but I could imagine how moved he and Mom were. I remembered the night in the dining room when I read the letter to Mom and we broke the "no tears" taboo and just let them flow.

Pastor Dan read John's letter in a heartfelt, tender way that perfectly expressed John's love and admiration of his father. The pastor's willingness to enter so graciously into our family's pain was a tribute to his compassion for the hospice patients he served.

I'm sure many in the room that day wondered why John was not at the funeral, after hearing his loving tribute to his father. The degree to which John expressed his love for Dad in the letter was the best he could do at that point in his life.

I knew Mom would have drawn great comfort had he been there, but she told me later she understood why he didn't come.

I knew my husband had prepared some remarks, but I hadn't read them. I was very moved by his words, and grateful that Paul was so fond of his father-in-law.

"When I married Kathleen, I had no idea how I would get along with Bob; but if I knew then what I know now, I would have relaxed a lot more from the very beginning," Paul said.

"Bob was a kind, thoughtful, and very entertaining person to be around. Being a talker myself, I appreciated Bob for his interest in everything from national politics, to the world of classical music. He was thoughtful and kind, and he never failed to ask how my own father was doing," Paul said.

My husband was eloquent. "Bob's true worth as a man was reflected in Kathleen's devotion to him, and her respect for his abilities and accomplishments."

He ended by summing up three messages he received from his father-in-law. "First, put in an honest day's work. Second, treat your family and friends with respect, and expect the same in return. Third, enjoy every day of your life, because no matter which card you've been dealt, there's something new and different about today." Paul finished his tribute and returned to his seat.

I was impressed with the poise of the grandchildren as they spoke about Grandpa Bob. Autumn, living the life of an artist in New York instead of getting married and having children, was a bit of a mystery to Dad, but he accepted her for who she was.

Autumn said, "Grandpa had a natural elegance. He carried himself with dignity and grace. He had taste. His craftsmanship was meticulous and durable. The last time I saw him he asked me to make him a masterpiece. He made me want to create something as beautiful and lasting as the things he made. He inspired me to be skilled and precise, like he was."

My daughter used very simple and poetic words to describe her Grandpa. Then she read a list of some of her memories of Grandpa that gave the assembled mourners a much-needed smile.

"I was terrified of being caught sitting in his chair," she began. Chuckles rose from the group, with nods from the other grandchildren. "Watching Lawrence Welk waltz in the bubbles. Staring at the power tools in awe and fear. Finally being old enough to join everyone for happy hour and Grandpa making me a Pink Lady. Teaching Grandpa the fine art of bowling, only to have him slip around on the lane in his wingtips. Finally, I remember when Grandpa and Grandma came to my show in Albuquerque."

The service did feel like a celebration, as Pastor Dan promised us, but it was also a goodbye—a painful, permanent, grief-drenched goodbye. I felt my Dad's presence in that old-fashioned room just as distinctly as I had smelled Old Spice aftershave in the bathroom after he left for work when I was a kid.

The last person to give a remembrance was Laura, one of Dad's home health aides. She knew him for a short amount of time, towards the end, and expressed her admiration for the way Dad handled his final days. Laura said she got to know Mr. Vallee as "Bob" and told us a common theme had recurred as she listened to Dad's family members speak: "character."

She encouraged us, the Vallee family, to carry on that theme in our lives.

I was surprised that a virtual stranger would praise our family in such glowing terms. I had always thought we were pretty dysfunctional and not very admirable. Laura came into our family circle and saw actions she admired. I was grateful that the last remembrance of my father was so eloquent.

Pastor Dan returned to the podium. "I wish," he said, "that I had gotten to know Bob Vallee at a different time. We probably wouldn't have talked much about religion . . . or politics (another chuckle from the mourners), but I appreciated the time I got to spend with him." Then he read a heartfelt poem.

"Some of you are familiar with this reading," Pastor Dan said. "It is entitled 'The Ship of Life,' written by John T. Baker."

> Along the shore I spy a ship
> As she sets out to sea;
> She spreads her sails and sniffs the breeze
> And slips away from me.
> I watch her fading image shrink,
> As she moves on and on,
> Until at last she's but a speck,
> Then someone says, "She's gone."
>
> Gone where? Gone only from our sight
> And from our farewell cries;
> That ship will somewhere reappear
> To other eager eyes.

Beyond the dim horizon's rim
Resound the welcome drums.
And while we're crying, "There she goes!"
They're shouting, "Here she comes!"

We're built to cruise for but a while
Upon this trackless sea
Until one day we sail away
Into infinity.

Pastor Dan sat down. We all remained in our seats until the recessional music began. Mom walked out first, looking as frail as a small bird, followed by Anne, me, and our husbands. We moved to the back of the room for cookies and coffee and received kind condolences from many people. Most had known Dad at the end of his life. I felt a sense of relief that the service was over. But more than that, I felt content that Dad's memorial was what he would have wanted it to be: short, dignified, not too religious, and sincere.

Anne caught my eye and motioned me over to the side porch. She held a container about the size of a shoebox with both hands. I looked at the box and then her face.

"Dad's ashes," she said in a hushed tone. "They're heavy."

"That's what's left of him?" I asked. "He always seemed so tall to me."

"I know," Anne said. "His physical presence is gone, that's for sure, but I felt his spirit during the service, didn't you?"

"Yes, absolutely," I said. "It meant a lot to Mom that the grandchildren spoke about Dad."

"They want us out of the room soon; another service is going to take place," Anne said as she put the box down on a table. We went to collect our mementos and began to leave, everyone carrying flowers, pictures, brochures, and the table Dad had made in high school. The funeral director discretely notified me that the next family was ready to begin setting up.

"Sis," Anne motioned me to come over to the reception area. "Go look at the portrait of the next guy," she said, directing me to the easel next to the parlor door. I took a few steps over, looked at a picture of an elderly man and went back to Anne.

"Who is he?" I asked.

"That's the guy who bought Mom and Dad's house on Stony Ridge Road." Anne was trying to whisper, but her body language was screaming.

"That's kind of creepy," I said. "The poor guy lived there for a year and a half, two years at the most. Mom and Dad had had twelve years to enjoy that beautiful home." With all our belongings loaded in the car, we left Ruffner-Wakelin and went back to Las Fuentes.

As with so many ceremonies that commemorate solemn events, as soon as the funeral was over, we quickly resumed our routines. Anne's friend, Diane, had lunch waiting for us when we returned to Las Fuentes. Autumn went back to Scottsdale with Anne's family to catch a flight to New York from the Phoenix airport. Ben, my son who so wisely advised me how to handle Mom just a few weeks ago, did what he had to do, which was the thankless job of driving a U-Haul truck with some of the heirlooms and furniture Dad had given me across the desert and back to California.

A few days after the funeral, Mom received a letter from Wanda, one of Dad's home health aides. She wanted to let Mom know that Dad had faced his last days with courage and accepted the help he needed from her and the other aides. She said she hoped her letter would provide us comfort. It did.

Dear Maryanne:

At the beautiful memorial service for your husband, Bob, we were asked to share our thoughts, but since I had seen him only three Thursday nights, I didn't feel qualified to share at that time. But after rethinking those nights, perhaps you would have some comfort from my observations, especially as they compare him so favorably with other hospice patients I have cared for.

I saw a man who was in control of himself and bore his responsibilities to his wife and children to the very end. He stayed as independent as possible, but when his weakness became too great, he submitted to our helping him in a gracious manner. That is not always the case with most men, but I have to share that in order for you to see the contrast. I didn't speak at the service because what I am about to tell you would not be appropriate in that setting.

I remember one man who was so withdrawn he would speak to no one but his wife. He would accept help from us, but in silence. Another man withdrew into childish dependency. Another one, who was used to "ruling the roost" with an angry spirit, continued that behavior to the extent of becoming physically violent and we had to sedate him to give him personal care.

Being weak was so hard for him that he finally pulled off the oxygen, refused all medications and help, and simply willed himself to die quickly. Another retreated into the past and talked as if he was in his office dealing with problems.

All these men are in stark contrast with the quiet, considerate, and gentlemanly manner that Bob Vallee handled his last days. He was truly a wonderful person.

May God bless you richly with His peace and comfort,

Wanda

The following week Anne and her husband held another ceremony at Paradise Garden's mausoleum in Scottsdale. Anne placed Dad's ashes in the niche that was purchased for Mom and him before he died. The mausoleum is a two-story building, open from floor to vaulted ceiling, giving it a lofty, airy feel. Clerestory windows at the top give the room a soft light, even on scorching hot summer days.

The building is dignified, but with a casual, Southwest ambiance. The focal point of the room is the bronze relief of a cowboy as seen from behind. He is hanging up his bridle, putting away his saddle, and finally going to rest. As does my father, he rests in peace.